THE ARTIFICIAL INTELLIGENCE HANDBOOK FOR GRAPHIC DESIGNERS

Future-Proof Your Skills; Save a Wealth of Time; and Secure Your Job.

Includes: 1000+ optimized ChatGPT Prompts & Strategies for Graphic Designers to Elevate Your Business Tasks and Innovate Successfully.

Author: Jeroen Erné

COPYRIGHT © 2023 BY JEROEN ERNÉ

Author: Jeroen Erné
Email: jeroen@nexibeo.com
Training Website: www.completeaitraining.com
Personal Website: www.jeroenerne.com
Business Website: www.nexibeo.com

First Edition: January, 2024

Self-Published by Jeroen Erné
Cover Design by: Jeroen Erné
Editor & Copy Editing by: The Nexibeo writers team

Disclaimer:
This book is designed to provide advice only on the subjects covered. While we try to specify the advice, information, and subjects specifically for your job function and job industry, there is no one-size-fits-all solution. No claims can be made based on the contents of this book. In the case you're looking for one-on-one personal training tailored for yourself or your

colleagues, general AI consultancy, or AI implementations, please contact the author via their email or website.

Dedication:
To those in the workforce who are committed to excellence, and who understand the pivotal role of artificial intelligence in shaping the future of employment. May this book serve as your guide to not just surviving, but thriving in a landscape forever transformed by technology.

INTRODUCTION

Welcome to "The Artificial Intelligence Handbook for Graphic Designers," a curated guide designed to navigate the intersection of artificial intelligence and graphic design. As you embark on this journey, prepare to uncover how ChatGPT and AI at large can become your creative allies, offering both inspiration and efficiency to your design process.

Within these pages lies a treasure trove of knowledge, with over 1000+ prompts to stimulate your creativity and streamline your workflow. Discover how ChatGPT can assist you from the inception of a design concept, based on detailed briefs or abstract goals, to the meticulous selection of fonts, colors, and layouts that resonate with your vision and your audience's expectations.

AI's role in graphic design is not to replace the designer but to augment your capabilities, providing insights into color theory, principles of layout, and brand identity development that resonate with your project's ethos. This handbook will guide you through interpreting client feedback intelligently, suggesting design adjustments, and managing digital assets effectively.

Moreover, delve into the nuances of creating platform-optimized graphics, understanding animation basics, and preparing designs for print with precision. As digital experiences become increasingly integral, gain insights into user interface design to craft intuitive and visually compelling interfaces.

Your portfolio is your story. Learn how to incorporate AI to showcase your range and skills, ensuring it reflects your unique voice and meets industry standards. Stay abreast of design trends with AI's analytical prowess, ensuring your work remains at the forefront of innovation.

This handbook is your mentor, speaking in an authoritative yet relatable tone, guiding you through the complexities of AI in graphic design with the finesse of an industry insider. Remember, this journey is about enhancing your creative expression and efficiency, preparing you to meet the ever-evolving demands of the graphic design world with confidence and curiosity. Welcome to the future of graphic design, where AI is your partner in creativity.

COMPLIMENTARY RESOURCES

If you purchase this book on Amazon or other book platforms, you will gain access to our complimentary resources. Here's a list of all the access you will receive:

☐ 1 month of complimentary access to CompleteAITraining.com, including:

☐ Access to our custom ChatGPTs tailored for your profession;

☐ Thousands of tailored prompts for your profession;

☐ All courses dedicated to training you to become an AI expert in your job;

☐ Unlimited questions to our AI strategy GPT.

☐ All video training materials;

☐ All audiobooks;

☐ All eBooks & reference guides;

You can request access to the complimentary resources at https://completeaitraining.com/free-resources-amazon .

WHAT IS CHATGPT?

ChatGPT is an AI chatbot by OpenAI that allows users to engage in "conversations" with it, designed to simulate natural dialogue. Users can pose questions or make requests using prompts, and ChatGPT will provide responses. This user-friendly, intuitive, and cost-free tool has quickly become a popular choice, serving as an alternative to conventional search engines and as a valuable resource for AI writing, among other applications.

What does"GPT" stand for?

The "GPT" in ChatGPT stands for generative pre-trained transformer. In AI, training involves teaching a computer system to recognize patterns and make decisions based on input data, similar to how a teacher imparts information to students and tests their understanding.

A transformer is a type of neural network trained to analyze the context of input data and weigh the significance of each part accordingly. This model learns context and is commonly used in natural language processing (NLP) to generate text similar to human writing.

In AI, a model consists of mathematical equations and algorithms that a computer uses to analyze data and make decisions. Unlike older AI chatbots, ChatGPT uses a dialog format, allowing it to answer follow-up and clarifying questions, as well as recognize and reject inappropriate or dangerous requests, such as questions about illegal activity.

HOW DOES CHATGPT WORK?

ChatGPT employs NLP, an AI tech that understands, analyzes, and generates human-like language. The LLM was trained using two inputs:

1. A huge volume of sample text from web pages and program code before 2021

2. Conversations from real humans, who showed desired responses to prompts, then ranked model outputs based on response quality

FEATURES AND LIMITATIONS OF CHATGPT AND OTHER GENERATIVE AI

ChatGPT is a groundbreaking leap in generative AI, offering numerous features that can expedite specific tasks when utilized strategically. However, it does have its constraints. Mastering both its capabilities and limitations is crucial for maximizing the potential of this technology.

FEATURES OF CHATGPT

ChatGPT can:
· Mimic the style and structure of input data
· Respond to prompts or input text, including storytelling or answering questions
· Generate text in multiple languages
· Modify the style of generated text (formal or informal)
· Ask clarifying questions to better understand input data
· Respond with text consistent with the context of a conversation, such as offering follow-up instructions or understanding references made to previous questions.

Other AI models can perform similar tasks with images, sounds, and video.

LIMITATIONS AND RISKS OF CHATGPT

While ChatGPT is a potent tool, it has its limitations. First, these transformer models lack common sense reasoning ability. This can lead to a limited capacity to handle complexity, nuance, and questions around emotions, values, beliefs, and abstract concepts. These limitations can manifest in various ways:

• It lacks understanding of the text it generates. While some output from ChatGPT may sound humanlike, the model isn't human. This has a few implications. It may have a limited ability to handle nuance, ambiguity, or things like sarcasm or irony. Perhaps more problematic is the fact that it can generate text that sounds plausible but is incorrect or even nonsensical. What's more, it can't verify the veracity of its output.

• It can produce biased, discriminatory, or offensive text. A language model like ChatGPT is only as good as its input data. This model was trained on large amounts of text data from across the internet, including biased input. If the data used to train the model is biased, this can show up in the generated text.

• Responses can be rooted in outdated information. The model has limited knowledge of events after 2021 and is not connected to the wider internet. If you're using ChatGPT to produce code, for example, it could be pulling from outdated examples that no longer meet modern cybersecurity standards.

• Output can be formulaic. ChatGPT can generate text

that's similar to existing text and is known to overuse certain phrases. This can mean text that reads as flat and unimaginative, or in more extreme cases, could constitute plagiarism or a copyright infringement.

• The tool isn't always available. The exploding popularity of ChatGPT has led to some capacity issues. When the servers get overloaded, you may get a message that "ChatGPT is at capacity."

CAN I USE CHAT GPT FOR FREE?

Absolutely, yes. OpenAI has indeed made ChatGPT available for free. However, it's important to note that the free version does come with certain limitations, particularly during peak usage times. It's worth mentioning that while ChatGPT may not remain free indefinitely, it currently serves as a valuable tool for OpenAI to gather user feedback and encourage widespread adoption of the AI language model across various sectors.

WHAT IS CHATGPT PLUS?

OpenAI has recently launched ChatGPT Plus, a subscription plan priced at $20 per month, offering faster response times, priority access to new features, improvements, and increased API usage limits. This plan is tailored to optimize your ChatGPT experience, ensuring the best possible results from your interactions with the chatbot.

GPT-3 VS GPT-3.5 VS GPT-4: WHAT DOES IT ALL MEAN?

GPT stands for "Generative Pre-trained Transformer." It's an AI language model developed by OpenAI. The term "Generative" refers to the model's ability to generate text based on input, while "Pre-trained" signifies that the model has been trained on a large dataset before being fine-tuned using human feedback and reinforcement learning. Finally, "Transformer" is the underlying architecture used in GPT, a neural network design introduced in 2017 that has become the foundation for many state-of-the-art natural language processing models. So, GPT is basically just the language model the ChatGPT AI bot uses to understand context and generate coherent, human-like text. The numbers that come after GPT like "GPT-3.5" or "GPT-4" simply refer to the model version number, with GPT-4 being the latest model of ChatGPT. While GPT-3 demonstrated impressive results in AI language processing, GPT-3.5 pushed the boundaries even further and incorporated improvements in both processing and output quality. However, GPT-4 goes even further and is much more concise than 3.5, so much so that it was able to pass the law bar exam with ease! Now that we've covered the nitty-gritty, we'll go over the exact steps to follow to start using ChatGPT in the next section.

SIGNING UP FOR CHATGPT

So you're ready to dive into ChatGPT? Great! This guide will walk you through every step. Don't worry, it's simple. Just make sure you have a browser like Google Chrome or Firefox, or really, any browser you like to use on your computer or phone.

Step 1: Head over to chat.openai.com. You'll see a "Sign up" button right there. Click it.

Welcome to ChatGPT

Log in with your OpenAI account to continue

Step 2: You'll see a form asking for your email and password. Fill it out. If you want to make it even easier, you can use your Google or Microsoft account to sign up.

Create your account

Please note that phone verification is required for signup. Your number will only be used to verify your identity for security purposes.

Email address

Continue

Already have an account? Log in

OR

G Continue with Google

Continue with Microsoft Account

Step 3: Before you move ahead, you've got to check your email to make sure it's really you. So, go ahead and open that verification email.

Verify your email

We sent an email to
█████@yahoo.com.
Click the link inside to get started.

Resend email

Step 4: Once you've verified your email, you'll be asked to give a few more details. Just basic stuff

Tell us about you

First name   Last name

Birthday (MM/DD/YYYY)

Continue

By clicking "Continue", you agree to our Terms and acknowledge our Privacy policy

Step 5: Almost there! Now they'll ask for your mobile number. You'll get a text with a code. Put that code in.

Verify your phone number

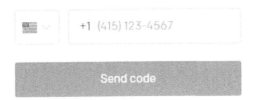

+1 (415) 123-4567

Send code

Step 6: Boom! You're in. Welcome to ChatGPT!

Quick heads-up: The free version of ChatGPT can sometimes be a bit slow or log you out if lots of people are using it. If you want to skip the line and make things smoother, you might want to look into getting the premium version. We'll talk about how to do that in the next section.

HOW TO SIGN UP FOR CHATGPT PLUS

If you're finding the free version of ChatGPT pretty neat but want to kick things up a notch—think faster replies, extra features, and first dibs on the cool new stuff—then ChatGPT Plus is what you're after. Upgrading is a cinch, and here's how to do it:

Step 1: Once you're logged in, look at the bottom-left corner of your dashboard. There's a button saying "Upgrade to Plus." Give it a click.

Step 2: You'll then see another button that says "Upgrade Plan." Go ahead, click it too.

Your plan   ✕

Free plan   **ChatGPT Plus** USD $20/mo

Your current plan   Upgrade plan

⊘ Available when demand is low   ⊘ Available even when demand is high

⊘ Standard response speed   ⊘ Faster response speed

⊘ Regular model updates   ⊘ Priority access to new features

                                  I need help with a billing issue

Now you'll go through the steps to put in your payment info and finish subscribing.

It's $20 a month, but what you get is more than worth it. Faster replies, no waiting—even during busy times—and you even get the latest from OpenAI, like the super-advanced GPT-4 model.

So, if you want the best experience ChatGPT has to offer, ChatGPT Plus is the way to go.

USING CHATGPT

Okay, you've got the hang of ChatGPT. This section will walk you through everything you need to know to maximize its potential and use ChatGPT efficiently, from crafting effective prompts to managing seamless back-and-forth dialogues.

WHAT IS A CHATGPT PROMPT?

OpenAI recently unveiled their latest ChatGPT system, a machine learning tool designed for natural language interaction. It has the ability to simulate human conversations and engage with people. As it is used more, ChatGPT improves its conversational skills and adapts to different messages. A ChatGPT prompt is a statement or question that starts a conversation with the AI assistant. It has been pre-trained on a wide range of data and can generate human-like responses to text prompts. Using natural language processing techniques, ChatGPT can understand and respond to prompts on various topics. The quality of the response depends on the topic and complexity of the prompt. The goal of a ChatGPT prompt is to initiate a friendly and engaging conversation with the AI assistant and obtain the desired information in a natural language format.

CHATGPT PERFECT PROMPT BASICS

Before diving into the specifics of crafting the ideal ChatGPT prompts, it's important to understand some general guidelines for creating effective prompts. Here are some tips to assist you in crafting the perfect prompt for ChatGPT:

- Focus on a clear and specific topic: Select a topic that aligns with your interests, inquiries, or objectives. Avoid broad or ambiguous topics to ensure the conversation remains focused and engaging.

- Use open-ended questions: Pose questions that encourage discussion and reflection. Avoid simple yes or no questions and instead ask questions that prompt thoughtful and detailed responses.

- Provide context: Offer background information to help the AI assistant or human responder grasp the purpose, scope, and goals of your prompt. This can lead to a more personalized and helpful response.

- Be courteous and respectful: ChatGPT is designed to foster a friendly and supportive conversation environment. Using respectful and polite language can cultivate a positive relationship with the assistant and improve the quality of the response.

- Use clear and concise language: Employ straightforward and concise language that is easy to comprehend. This can prevent misunderstandings and make it easier for the chatbot or human responder to provide a relevant and helpful response.

By adhering to these guidelines, you can craft a perfect prompt for ChatGPT that is relevant, engaging, and focused.

WRITE PERFECT PROMPTS FOR CHATGPT IN 5 SIMPLE STEPS

Are you prepared to enhance your ChatGPT experience? The secret lies in mastering the art of prompt writing. This section covers the fundamentals in five straightforward, actionable steps. But that's just the beginning. In the later chapters, we'll furnish you with a thorough catalog of prompts, carefully tailored to your particular role and sector. So, stay tuned; we're not just enhancing your ChatGPT interaction—we're striving for a revolutionary change.

1. Narrow down your topic

When crafting the perfect ChatGPT prompt, follow these steps:

• Generate ideas: Begin by brainstorming broad themes or topics that pique your interest. This could range from sports, music, or travel to technology, health, or finance.

• Pinpoint specific topics: Then, pinpoint specific topics or sub-topics within the broader theme that you wish to delve into. For instance, if your broad theme is technology, you might narrow it down to artificial intelligence, cybersecurity, or social media.

• Consider the audience: Take into account your target audience and the topics they are likely to find compelling or pertinent. This can aid in selecting a topic that will captivate your audience and elicit more informative and insightful responses.

• Research the topic: Thoroughly research your chosen topic to ensure that you possess sufficient knowledge to pose informed and relevant questions.

• Define the scope: Lastly, define the scope of the prompt to ensure that it is specific and focused. Avoid broad or vague prompts that may be challenging for the AI assistant to interpret.

2. Use action words

Using action words to craft the ideal ChatGPT prompt is crucial for clarity, specificity, and engagement. These words convey the prompt's purpose and prompt the AI assistant to deliver more informative and insightful responses. Here's a list of action words for crafting the perfect ChatGPT prompts:

• Identify
• Describe
• Explain
• Compare
• Contrast
• Discuss
• Analyze
• Evaluate
• Recommend
• Suggest
• Propose
• Predict
• Assess
• Interpret
• Apply
• Demonstrate
• Illustrate
• Elaborate

• Justify
• Validate

3. Provide context for the AI

Providing context for your topic when crafting the perfect ChatGPT prompt is crucial. It helps the AI assistant grasp the background, purpose, and scope of the prompt. Here are some tips:
• Define your topic clearly and concisely to ensure the AI assistant understands the focus.
• Provide additional details like history, current status, and future trends to give the AI assistant more context.
• Explain why the topic is relevant to you and why you want to discuss it with the AI assistant.
• Outline the goals or objectives of the prompt so the AI assistant knows what information you're seeking.
• Use supporting examples or anecdotes to illustrate your topic and provide more context and detail.

4. Define what output you want

To save time, clearly define the desired output for ChatGPT in your prompt. Consider these key aspects:
• Tone: Formal, informal, friendly, or professional.
• Language: Specify the language.
• Length: Short, paragraph, or longer response.
• Format: Text, audio, or video.
• Detail: Level of detail needed.
• Personalization: Level of personalization desired.

5. Interact with the AI

When crafting the ideal ChatGPT prompt, it's crucial to know how to engage with ChatGPT after initiating a chat for the best response. Here are some tips:
• Ask Follow-Up Questions: Seek more details on specific parts of the response with targeted follow-up questions to refine and

clarify.

• Refine Answers: If the response isn't quite what you need, provide feedback and refine the question or prompt for a more accurate response.

• Clarify: If the response is unclear, ask for clarification to ensure a more precise and tailored response.

• Provide Feedback: Personalize future interactions and improve responses by giving feedback on the quality and relevance of the response.

• Specify: Direct the AI to be more specific about intent or purpose in the conversation to receive the desired response.

• Stay Engaged: Keep the conversation going with relevant questions, maintaining an informative dialogue, and providing feedback throughout the interaction.

By following these tips, you can write better prompts for ChatGPT and train your interactions with the AI chatbot for more efficient results!

EXAMPLES OF BAD CHATGPT PROMPTS

Here are some examples of bad ChatGPT prompts:

- "Tell me anything you know." – This is an overly broad prompt that does not provide any specific information or context for the AI assistant to work with.
- "I don't know what to ask. What do you want to talk about?" – This prompt puts the burden of the conversation solely on the AI assistant, rather than providing direction or context.
- "Can you write me a story?" – This prompt is too vague and does not provide specific details or context for the AI assistant to work with.
- "Do my homework." – This is unethical, inappropriate, and doesn't encourage the AI assistant to provide insightful or meaningful responses.
- "What color am I thinking of?" – This prompt is meaningless and irrelevant, does not provide any feedback or learnings from the interaction.
- "Talk to me about nothing." – This prompt is not constructive, vague, and irrelevant— the AI assistant can't initiate an engaging conversation without any context to draw from.
- "Why are you so dumb?" – This is an inappropriate and disrespectful prompt that won't enable engagement with the AI assistant.

In general, bad ChatGPT prompts are overly general or vague, lack context or clarity, use inappropriate language, or simply irrelevant to engage the AI assistant. The prompts need to be focused, clear, and appropriate to generate valuable insights and learning.

EXAMPLES OF GOOD CHATGPT PROMPTS

Here are some examples of effective ChatGPT prompts:
• "Explain zero waste practices and how individuals can incorporate them into their daily lives."
• "Recommend innovative technologies, tools, and best practices to improve supply chain processes and minimize waste."
• "How can businesses use data analytics to better understand customer needs and improve sales and marketing outcomes?"
• "Share examples of how Machine Learning models are used in the healthcare industry to improve diagnosis, treatment, and patient outcomes."
• "How can we enhance environmental sustainability in the production and distribution of food? What initiatives and policies would be most effective in bringing about change?"
• "What are the pros and cons of remote work, and what practices should companies implement to ensure its success?"
• Effective ChatGPT prompts are focused, specific, and encourage detailed engagement from the AI assistant. They provide enough background, context, and direction for the AI assistant to develop an informative and insightful response. They also aim to solve real-world problems rather than asking meaningless questions.

WHAT ARE CHATGPT CUSTOM INSTRUCTIONS?

Custom Instructions enable you to personalize your ChatGPT interactions, ensuring the model reflects your unique tone, style, and expertise. Instead of relying solely on its broad database, ChatGPT takes direct guidance from you for its responses.

This feature also eliminates the need to repeatedly input or copy-paste important details and preferences each time you use ChatGPT. Custom Instructions enforce your guidelines, writing style, and instructions, optimizing your interactions and saving you time.

At a fundamental level, Custom Instructions can maintain the same voice and style for blog posts, emails, and marketing materials. For those in development and programming roles, Custom Instructions allow you to direct ChatGPT to generate code in a consistent, unified style.

For example, a teacher can create a lesson plan without constantly mentioning that they're teaching 3rd-grade science. Similarly, a developer aiming for efficient code in Python can state their preference just once, and ChatGPT will consistently consider this.

HOW DO I USE CUSTOM INSTRUCTIONS?

Utilizing ChatGPT's Custom Instructions for content creation is a simple process with significant benefits. Whether crafting blog posts, social media content, or marketing materials, custom guidelines can streamline your workflow and enhance the quality of your output.

STEPS TO ACTIVATE CHATGPT CUSTOM INSTRUCTIONS

Below the 2 quick steps on how to set up ChatGPT custom Instructions.

Step 1. Click the three dots next to your name and select "Custom instructions."

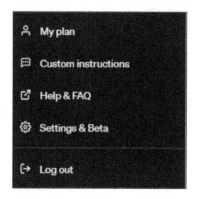

Step 2. Set up custom instructions

If you're looking for ChatGPT to function in a specific role, you can indicate that in your custom instructions. Here's how you could add that element:

"ChatGPT, act as a job function assistant, focusing on administrative tasks. Please respond in a formal tone, summarizing your thoughts in bullet points. Keep your responses concise and within 100 words. Confirm your understanding of our mission and vision before proceeding with the conversation."

In this example, specifying "act as a job function assistant focusing on administrative tasks" gives ChatGPT a role to play, guiding the nature of its responses to fit within the scope of typical administrative assistance. This can be particularly useful if you want the conversation to focus on a specific set of tasks or functions.

Besides that you can set custom instructions for how you would like ChatGPT to respond, you could specify things like tone, format, or any special requirements. Here are some examples:

- Tone: "Please respond in a formal/business tone."
- Format: "Summarize your responses in bullet points."
- Depth: "Provide detailed explanations for any technical terms used."
- Length: "Keep responses concise, not exceeding 100 words."
- Interactivity: "Ask follow-up questions to clarify any unclear points."
- Focus: "Please focus on the practical applications of our offerings."
- Verification: "Confirm your understanding of our mission and vision before proceeding."

So a custom instruction could look something like:
"ChatGPT, please respond in a formal tone, summarizing your thoughts in bullet points. Keep your responses concise and within 100 words. Confirm your understanding of our mission and vision before proceeding with the conversation."

Example custom instructions for: "What would you like ChatGPT to know about you to provide better responses?"

In order to receive more personalized and accurate responses from ChatGPT, you might consider providing some background information or specifying your preferences and needs. Here's how you could phrase those custom instructions:

Prompt:
Hello, ChatGPT. Meet [Company Name]—our mission is to [Business Mission] and our vision is [Business Vision]. We are in the [industry], and we specialize in [brief description].

Key USPs:
[USP 1]
[USP 2]
[USP 3]

KPIs we track:
[KPI 1]
[KPI 2]
[KPI 3]

Our offerings:
[Product/Service 1]: [Brief Benefit]
[Product/Service 2]: [Brief Benefit]
[Product/Service 3]: [Brief Benefit]

Please confirm your understanding and keep these details in mind for our conversation. Feel free to ask questions.
Note that custom instructions fields can contain a maximum of 1500 characters.

Example custom instructions for: "How would you like ChatGPT to respond?"

If you're looking for ChatGPT to function in a specific role, you can indicate that in your custom instructions. Here's how you could add that element:

"ChatGPT, act as a job function assistant, focusing on administrative tasks. Please respond in a formal tone, summarizing your thoughts in bullet points. Keep your responses concise and within 100 words. Confirm your understanding of our mission and vision before proceeding with the conversation."

In this example, specifying "act as a job function assistant focusing on administrative tasks" gives ChatGPT a role to play, guiding the nature of its responses to fit within the scope of typical administrative assistance. This can be particularly useful if you want the conversation to focus on a specific set of tasks or functions."

Besides that you can set custom instructions for how you would like ChatGPT to respond, you could specify things like tone, format, or any special requirements. Here are some examples:
• Tone: "Please respond in a formal/business tone."
• Format: "Summarize your responses in bullet points."
• Depth: "Provide detailed explanations for any technical terms used."
• Length: "Keep responses concise, not exceeding 100 words."
• Interactivity: "Ask follow-up questions to clarify any unclear points."
• Focus: "Please focus on the practical applications of our offerings."
• Verification: "Confirm your understanding of our mission and vision before proceeding."

So a custom instruction could look something like:
"ChatGPT, please respond in a formal tone, summarizing your thoughts in bullet points. Keep your responses concise and within 100 words. Confirm your understanding of our mission and vision before proceeding with the conversation."

CHATGPT'S ADVANCED DATA ANALYSIS FEATURE - ANALYSE DATA WITHIN MINUTES.

CHATGPT ADVANCED DATA ANALYSIS UNVEILED

In the expansive, ever-changing realm of AI, we must familiarize ourselves with the groundbreaking ChatGPT's Advanced Data Analysis tool. We are about to embark on a journey that goes beyond mere text generation, delving into a domain where running code, solving complex problems, and effortlessly managing file uploads and downloads becomes the standard. The future, my friends, is not some distant tomorrow – it is here today. Let us welcome it with ChatGPT's Advanced Data Analysis, and allow me to lead you through its remarkable capabilities.

TRANSCENDING THE STANDARD CHATGPT LIMITATIONS

In a world where AI constantly reshapes the tech scene, ChatGPT stands as a symbol of innovation. However, it has encountered limitations - grappling with math problems, unable to generate or interpret images, and contending with hallucinated responses. But those days are over. With Advanced Data Analysis, picture a realm where you can effortlessly execute all of the above and more with finesse and accuracy.

A DATA ANALYST
SITTING NEXT TO YOU

Do not fear the complexity, for even the most cutting-edge tools have their origins in simplicity. Advanced Data Analysis, previously known as the Code Interpreter, is a source of optimism, elevating ChatGPT's capabilities to conduct mathematical computations, analyze data, interpret Python code, and much more. Therefore, do not fret about the complexities, because with Advanced Data Analysis, you are in secure, capable hands.

ACTIVATING ADVANCED DATA ANALYSIS IN CHATGPT

Turning on the Advanced Data Analysis is simple.

Please note, this feature is only available in the paid version of ChatGPT Plus.

If you have an account, just follow these steps:
1. Logging In: Easily sign in to your ChatGPT Plus account.
2. Navigating to Settings: Head to the settings page. This is your control center in ChatGPT.

3. Selecting the Beta Option: Choose "Beta." You'll see various options here, including the Advanced Data Analysis.

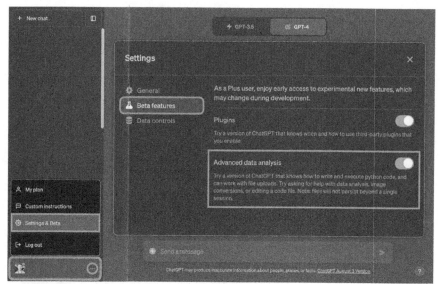

4. Activation: Just click to activate the Advanced Data Analysis plugin, like flipping on a light switch.

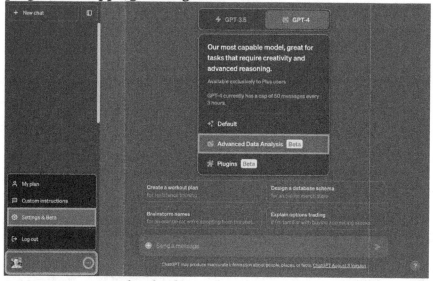

5. Now you can upload a file.

6. Select any file you want to use from your computer.

7. And now you can interact with that file. You can make new versions, data visualisations, analaysis. etc.

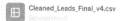

Advanced Data Analysis

 Cleaned_Leads_Final_v4.csv
Spreadsheet

Make a new CSV with new leads from the Restaurant Industry and only add CEOs, General Directors and Founders to the new sheet.

 To begin processing the CSV file and extracting leads from the Restaurant Industry with titles of CEOs, General Directors, and Founders, let's first load the CSV file and examine its contents. This will help us understand the structure of the data and identify the relevant columns for filtering the leads. Shall we proceed?

↻ Regenerate

⊕ Yes

PRACTICAL EXAMPLES

Imagine the possibilities as vast as the cosmos with ChatGPT's Advanced Data Analysis. Picture yourself uploading data, generating impactful visualizations, and retrieving the results with effortless grace, all while wielding a reservoir of formidable power at your fingertips. Analyze extensive datasets, create charts, identify anomalies, and make informed decisions based on precise, reliable data, all in just moments. The power to unlock these potentials firmly resides within your reach, waiting to be unleashed.

Uploadable File Types:
- Text Files (.txt, .csv, .json, .xml, etc.)
- Image Files (.jpg, .png, .gif, etc.)
- Document Files (.pdf, .docx, .xlsx, .pptx, etc.)
- Code Files (.py, .js, .html, .css, etc.)
- Data Files (.csv, .xlsx, .tsv, .json, etc.)
- Audio Files (.mp3, .wav, etc.)
- Video Files (.mp4, .avi, .mov, etc.)

The Analysis possibilities.
Engage in a multitude of tasks and analysis when you upload your chosen file type:

- File Transformation: Seamlessly transition between file types, merging and converting as needed.
- Inquisitive Analysis: Question your data, uncovering hidden layers and invaluable insights.
- Advanced Analytics: Navigate through the depths of your data, exploring trends, patterns, and data-driven pathways for

decision making.

- Data Visualization: Bring your data to life with vibrant, clear, and informative visuals, enhancing understanding and interpretation.

- Anomaly Detection: Identify and analyze anomalies within your data, providing clarity and ensuring data reliability.

- Predictive Analytics: Harness your data to anticipate and prepare for future trends and events.

- Text Analysis: Delve into textual data for sentiment analysis, keyword extraction, and more, revealing the sentiments and themes within.

- Image and Video Analysis: Extract valuable information from images and videos, analyzing content, patterns, and features.

JOURNEY AHEAD

In the upcoming chapters, we will delve into the myriad tasks achievable with Advanced Data Analysis prompts. These guides will lead you through the complex realm of advanced data analytics with confidence and precision.

The future doesn't wait, but with Advanced Data Analysis, you're not simply progressing towards it; you're beckoning the future towards you.

USING AI TO CREATE YOUR VISUALS (PHOTO'S, IMAGES, ART ETC)

Crafting visually captivating and pertinent imagery has always been a pivotal aspect of storytelling, marketing, and conveying intricate concepts. The emergence of artificial intelligence (AI) has significantly broadened the scope of image creation. AI now empowers us to produce lifelike images, 3D renders, cartoons, explainer visuals, and descriptive imagery with remarkable ease, revolutionizing what was once a laborious task. Two standout AI tools in this domain are Midjourney and DALL-E.

Midjourney
Midjourney stands as a generative AI program and service developed and hosted by the independent research lab Midjourney, Inc. based in San Francisco. This innovative tool generates images from natural language descriptions, known as "prompts", effortlessly transforming textual input into a diverse array of image styles. Whether it's a lifelike image of a tranquil landscape, a 3D render of a complex architectural design, or a simple cartoon for a children's book, Midjourney makes such creative pursuits easily accessible. Explore Midjourney: https://www.midjourney.com.

DALL-E

DALL-E, DALL-E 2, and DALL-E 3 are text-to-image models crafted by OpenAI using deep learning techniques to produce digital images from natural language descriptions, known as "prompts". With a simple text prompt, these models can generate a variety of images, from lifelike visuals and stylized cartoons to intricate 3D renders. For example, a prompt like "a futuristic city skyline" could result in a finely detailed 3D render or a stylized cartoon, depending on the specified parameters. Explore DALL-E: https://openai.com/dall-e-2.

The journey of creating images using AI tools like DALL-E and the envisioned Midjourney, while brimming with boundless creative possibilities, may come with a learning curve. For video tutorials on how to harness these AI tools for image creation, you can refer to jeroenerne.com/AI-images. This resource offers a visual guide that can aid in comprehending and navigating the process of AI-assisted image generation, streamlining the journey from textual description to visual representation.

CHATGPT FOR GRAPHIC DESIGNERSS

Welcome to this guide tailored for Graphic Designerss. If you're looking to boost efficiency and creativity, you're in the right place. This guide will introduce you to ChatGPT, an AI-powered tool that will become your essential ally.

What's Coming Up
In the upcoming chapters, we'll explore specific tasks that define your role. Each chapter will offer precise instructions and custom prompts to help you tackle the unique challenges of your industry and job.

Customized Prompts for Your Role
You'll discover over 1000 carefully curated prompts to assist you with everything from daily tasks to complex projects. This isn't a one-size-fits-all solution; it's a targeted toolkit to enhance your day-to-day work. As a reader, you can request a document with all these prompts via https://jeroenerne.com/prompt/ for easy access.

DESIGN CONCEPT
DEVELOPMENT

THE GENESIS OF DESIGN: CONCEPT DEVELOPMENT

In the realm of graphic design, the ever-evolving landscape of technology continually reshapes the way we approach creative processes. Among the transformative forces at play, Artificial Intelligence (AI) has emerged as a powerful tool that can aid graphic designers in their mission to craft visually compelling narratives. In this chapter, we will explore how ChatGPT can seamlessly integrate into your design workflow, offering invaluable assistance in the realm of design concept development.

Imagine a scenario where Lisa, a seasoned graphic designer, receives a new client brief. The client, an up-and-coming tech startup, seeks a striking visual identity for their cutting-edge product launch. The challenge? The client's product, a revolutionary AI-powered software, requires a design concept that communicates innovation, sophistication, and approachability. Lisa faces the daunting task of translating these abstract ideas into a tangible visual language.

Here's where ChatGPT steps in as a trusted ally. With its unparalleled natural language understanding capabilities, ChatGPT can help Lisa brainstorm and develop design concepts that align perfectly with the client's vision. By feeding it the key attributes and goals provided in the brief, Lisa kickstarts a dynamic conversation with this AI-driven tool.

"ChatGPT, I need a design concept that embodies innovation, sophistication, and approachability," Lisa begins. "The client's product is a game-changer in the AI industry, and they want our design to reflect that."

Within seconds, ChatGPT responds with thoughtful suggestions. "Certainly, Lisa. To convey innovation, consider incorporating sleek, futuristic elements into your design, such as clean lines and metallic accents. Sophistication can be represented through a refined color palette and a minimalist layout. To add a touch of approachability, maybe incorporate friendly, inviting icons or characters."

Lisa is impressed by the initial guidance provided by ChatGPT. She appreciates how the AI understands the nuances of her project and provides actionable insights tailored to her specific needs. This allows her to dive deeper into her design exploration with newfound confidence.

As Lisa delves further into the conversation with ChatGPT, she refines her ideas and receives valuable suggestions that fuel her creative process. The AI recommends potential color schemes, font choices, and even imagery concepts that align with the project's objectives. ChatGPT also provides historical design references that incorporate AI symbolism, ensuring that Lisa's work remains relevant and on-trend.

What sets ChatGPT apart in design concept development is its ability to adapt and iterate in real-time. Lisa can request variations, discuss design elements in greater detail, or even explore the emotional impact of different visual choices. Through this interactive dialogue, ChatGPT becomes an indispensable partner in the creative journey.

Lisa ultimately crafts a design concept that not only meets but exceeds her client's expectations. The visual identity she presents encapsulates the essence of innovation, sophistication, and approachability, all while staying true to the AI-driven nature of the product. Her client is thrilled, and Lisa credits ChatGPT for playing a pivotal role in this success.

In conclusion, the integration of ChatGPT into the graphic design process empowers professionals like Lisa to elevate their work to new heights. By leveraging the AI's ability to brainstorm, refine, and adapt design concepts based on client briefs and creative goals, designers can unlock a world of possibilities. With ChatGPT as your design ally, you're not just designing; you're orchestrating a symphony of creativity that resonates with your audience and delivers tangible results. So, embrace the power of AI in design concept development, and let your creativity flourish as never before.

Task: Mood board creation

Gathering visual inspiration and references for a design concept

Example Prompt 1:
Create a mood board for a modern, minimalist design concept using images that evoke simplicity and clean lines.

Example Prompt 2:

Gather visual inspiration for a vintage-inspired design concept, incorporating images of retro typography, color palettes, and textures.

Example Prompt 3:

Curate a mood board for a nature-inspired design concept, featuring images of organic textures, earthy tones, and natural elements.

Example Prompt 4:

Collect visual references for a futuristic design concept, including images of sleek technology, metallic textures, and bold, futuristic typography.

Task: Color palette selection

Choosing a cohesive and effective color scheme for a design

Example Prompt 1:

Can you suggest a color palette that conveys a sense of modernity and sophistication for a corporate branding project?

Example Prompt 2:

What colors would work best for a nature-inspired design, evoking a sense of tranquility and harmony?

Example Prompt 3:

I'm looking for a color scheme that captures the energy and excitement of a music festival - what combinations do you recommend?

Example Prompt 4:

How can I create a cohesive color palette for a website design that balances professionalism with creativity?

Task: Typography exploration

Finding suitable fonts and type treatments for a design

concept

Example Prompt 1:
Can you suggest some modern and sleek fonts that would work well for a minimalist design concept?

Example Prompt 2:
I'm looking for a font that conveys a sense of elegance and sophistication for a luxury brand - any recommendations?

Example Prompt 3:
What are some unique and eye-catching type treatments that could be used for a bold and edgy design concept?

Example Prompt 4:
I need a font that balances professionalism with creativity for a corporate branding project - any ideas for a versatile typeface?

Task: Visual style research

Investigating different visual styles and trends for a design project

Example Prompt 1:
Can you provide examples of contemporary graphic design styles that incorporate minimalist elements and bold typography?

Example Prompt 2:
I'm looking for inspiration from retro design trends, particularly from the 1960s and 1970s. Can you suggest some visual styles or specific design elements that were popular during that time?

Example Prompt 3:
I'm interested in exploring the use of vibrant colors and geometric patterns in my design project. Can you recommend any current visual trends or design movements that incorporate these elements?

Example Prompt 4:
I'm curious about the intersection of digital and traditional art

styles in graphic design. Can you share any examples of visual styles that blend hand-drawn elements with digital techniques?

Task: Image sourcing

Finding and selecting appropriate images or graphics to complement a design concept

Example Prompt 1:
Can you help me find high-quality, royalty-free images of nature scenes for a project I'm working on?

Example Prompt 2:
I'm looking for abstract graphics that convey a sense of creativity and innovation. Can you suggest some sources or keywords to search for?

Example Prompt 3:
I need images of diverse people engaging in various activities for a promotional campaign. Where can I find a wide range of inclusive and representative visuals?

Example Prompt 4:
I'm designing a website for a travel company and need striking photos of popular destinations. Any recommendations for image libraries or stock photo websites with a good selection?

Task: Concept sketching

Brainstorming and sketching initial ideas for a design concept

Example Prompt 1:
Create a rough sketch of a logo concept that incorporates elements of nature and technology for a sustainable energy company.

Example Prompt 2:
Brainstorm and sketch out initial ideas for a website layout that conveys a sense of adventure and exploration for a travel agency.

Example Prompt 3:

Design a concept sketch for a product packaging that combines minimalist aesthetics with bold, eye-catching typography for a new skincare line.

Example Prompt 4:
Brainstorm and sketch initial ideas for a poster design that promotes a music festival, incorporating elements of retro and modern design styles.

Task: Design feedback analysis

Gathering and analyzing feedback on design concepts to refine and improve them

Example Prompt 1:
Can you provide specific feedback on the color scheme and how it complements the overall design concept?

Example Prompt 2:
What are your thoughts on the typography choices and how they contribute to the overall visual appeal and readability of the design?

Example Prompt 3:
Please share any suggestions for improving the layout and composition of the design to enhance user experience and visual impact.

Example Prompt 4:
How does the design concept align with the brand's identity and messaging? Any recommendations for strengthening this connection?

Task: Design presentation preparation

Creating visual materials and presentations to showcase design concepts to clients or stakeholders

Example Prompt 1:

Create a visually engaging presentation template that incorporates our brand colors and design elements to use for showcasing design concepts to clients.

Example Prompt 2:
Design a series of infographics to visually communicate key design concepts and data points for our upcoming stakeholder presentation.

Example Prompt 3:
Develop a set of mockups and visual prototypes to demonstrate the user experience and interface design for our new product, to be included in our presentation to stakeholders.

Example Prompt 4:
Produce a series of visually compelling case studies highlighting our past design projects, to be used as part of our portfolio presentation to potential clients.

Idea: Mood board creation

ChatGPT can help generate ideas for color schemes, typography, and visual elements to create a mood board for design inspiration.

Example Prompt 1:
Hey ChatGPT, I'm working on a new project and need some inspiration for a mood board. Can you help me brainstorm color schemes, typography, and visual elements that would work well together to create a cohesive and inspiring design?

Example Prompt 2:
I'm feeling stuck on creating a mood board for a client presentation. Can you assist me in generating ideas for color palettes, font pairings, and visual elements that will convey the right mood and aesthetic for the project?

Example Prompt 3:
I'm looking to revamp my portfolio and want to start with a mood

board to gather design inspiration. Can you provide suggestions for color combinations, typography styles, and visual elements that will help me create a visually appealing and cohesive mood board?

Example Prompt 4:
I'm in the early stages of a new branding project and need help developing a mood board to guide the design direction. Can you assist me in brainstorming color schemes, font choices, and visual elements that will capture the essence of the brand and resonate with the target audience?

Idea: Brainstorming design concepts

ChatGPT can assist in generating creative ideas and concepts for design projects.

Example Prompt 1:
Hey ChatGPT, I need some fresh ideas for a new logo design. Can you help me brainstorm some creative concepts that capture the essence of our brand?

Example Prompt 2:
I'm working on a website redesign and I'm looking for some innovative design concepts. Can you assist me in brainstorming ideas that will make our website stand out?

Example Prompt 3:
I'm in the process of creating a new product packaging design and I could use some help generating unique and eye-catching concepts. Can you provide some creative ideas to inspire my design process?

Example Prompt 4:
I'm working on a marketing campaign and I need some out-of-the-box design concepts to grab people's attention. Can you help me brainstorm some creative ideas that will make our campaign memorable?

Idea: Design trend research

ChatGPT can provide insights into current design trends and help in staying updated with the latest design concepts.

Example Prompt 1:
Can you provide a summary of the latest design trends in web and app design, including color schemes, typography, and layout styles?

Example Prompt 2:
I'm looking to stay ahead of the curve in graphic design. Can you help me identify emerging trends in logo and branding design?

Example Prompt 3:
I'm interested in understanding the current trends in packaging design for consumer products. Can you provide insights into popular styles and visual elements?

Example Prompt 4:
I need to update my portfolio with the latest design trends. Can you help me identify popular design styles in print and digital media?

Idea: Concept sketching

ChatGPT can assist in generating initial sketches and rough concepts for design projects.

Example Prompt 1:
Create a series of rough concept sketches for a new logo design, incorporating elements of nature and technology.

Example Prompt 2:
Assist in brainstorming and sketching out initial ideas for a website layout that emphasizes user-friendly navigation and modern aesthetics.

Example Prompt 3:
Help generate rough concept sketches for a packaging design that

conveys a sense of luxury and sustainability.

Example Prompt 4:
Collaborate on creating initial concept sketches for a social media campaign, focusing on vibrant colors and engaging visual elements.

Idea: Design concept testing

ChatGPT can help in creating surveys or questionnaires to gather feedback on design concepts from potential users or clients.

Example Prompt 1:
Create a survey template for gathering feedback on a new logo design concept. Include questions about overall appeal, clarity, and brand alignment.

Example Prompt 2:
Develop a questionnaire to gather user feedback on a website redesign concept. Ask about ease of navigation, visual appeal, and overall user experience.

Example Prompt 3:
Design a feedback form for testing a new packaging design concept. Include questions about shelf appeal, product recognition, and purchase intent.

Example Prompt 4:
Create a survey to gather client feedback on a new advertising campaign concept. Include questions about message clarity, visual impact, and brand representation.

Idea: Iterative design concept development

ChatGPT can assist in refining and iterating on design concepts based on feedback and insights.

Example Prompt 1:

ChatGPT, I need your help in refining and iterating on a logo design concept. Can you provide insights and suggestions for improving the overall aesthetic and messaging of the design?

Example Prompt 2:

I'm working on a website layout and I'd like ChatGPT to assist in refining the design concept. Can you provide feedback on the user experience and suggest improvements for the overall visual appeal?

Example Prompt 3:

As a graphic designer, I'm looking to iterate on a packaging design concept. Can ChatGPT provide insights and suggestions for enhancing the visual impact and functionality of the design?

Example Prompt 4:

I need assistance in refining and iterating on a branding concept. Can ChatGPT help in providing feedback and ideas for improving the overall cohesiveness and uniqueness of the design?

Idea: Design concept presentation

ChatGPT can help in creating visually appealing presentations to showcase design concepts to clients or stakeholders.

Example Prompt 1:

Create a visually stunning presentation template that incorporates our brand colors and design elements to showcase our latest design concept to potential clients.

Example Prompt 2:

Help us design a series of slides that effectively communicate the inspiration, process, and final vision behind our latest design concept to present to our stakeholders.

Example Prompt 3:

Assist in creating a dynamic and engaging presentation that includes interactive elements to showcase our design concept in a unique and memorable way to our audience.

Example Prompt 4:
Collaborate with us to develop a visually appealing and cohesive presentation that effectively communicates the key features and benefits of our design concept to our target audience.

Idea: Design concept prototyping

ChatGPT can assist in creating interactive prototypes to visualize and test design concepts.

Example Prompt 1:
Create a series of interactive wireframes for a new mobile app concept, incorporating user flows and interactive elements to demonstrate the functionality and user experience.

Example Prompt 2:
Assist in designing a web-based prototype for a new e-commerce platform, including interactive product pages, checkout process, and user account management.

Example Prompt 3:
Help in visualizing a virtual reality experience by creating interactive mockups of the environment, user interactions, and immersive elements.

Example Prompt 4:
Support in prototyping a new interactive digital dashboard for data visualization, including dynamic charts, filters, and real-time data updates.

Idea: Design concept storytelling

ChatGPT can help in crafting compelling narratives and stories around design concepts to communicate their purpose and value.

Example Prompt 1:
Prompt: "ChatGPT, can you help me craft a compelling narrative

around a new logo design concept? I want to communicate the purpose and value of the logo through a captivating story that resonates with our audience."

Example Prompt 2:
Prompt: "I need assistance in creating a storytelling campaign for our latest product design concept. Can ChatGPT help me in crafting a narrative that effectively communicates the innovative features and benefits of the design to our target customers?"

Example Prompt 3:
Prompt: "ChatGPT, I'm looking to develop a narrative around our upcoming website redesign concept. Can you assist me in crafting a story that highlights the user experience improvements and the overall value that the new design will bring to our visitors?"

Example Prompt 4:
Prompt: "I'm working on a design concept for a new packaging design, and I need help in storytelling to convey the brand's identity and the unique selling points of the product. Can ChatGPT support me in creating a narrative that captures the essence of the design and its value to consumers?"

Idea: Design concept evaluation
ChatGPT can assist in evaluating the effectiveness and feasibility of design concepts based on various criteria.

Example Prompt 1:
Hey ChatGPT, I'm working on a new design concept for a website layout. Can you help me evaluate its effectiveness in terms of user experience, visual appeal, and functionality?

Example Prompt 2:
ChatGPT, I need your assistance in evaluating the feasibility of a new logo design concept for a client. Can you provide insights on its scalability, versatility, and brand representation?

Example Prompt 3:

I'm brainstorming a packaging design concept for a new product. Can ChatGPT help me assess its effectiveness in terms of shelf appeal, information hierarchy, and consumer engagement?

Example Prompt 4:
ChatGPT, I'm exploring a new design concept for a mobile app interface. Can you assist me in evaluating its usability, accessibility, and overall user satisfaction?

Idea: Design concept collaboration

ChatGPT can facilitate collaboration and idea-sharing among team members to develop design concepts collectively.

Example Prompt 1:
Hey ChatGPT, can you help facilitate a brainstorming session for our design team to collaborate on a new concept for our upcoming project? We need to generate ideas and share feedback in real-time.

Example Prompt 2:
ChatGPT, we're looking to crowdsource design concepts from our team members. Can you assist in creating a platform for everyone to contribute their ideas and provide feedback to each other?

Example Prompt 3:
We're in need of a virtual whiteboard where our design team can sketch out their concepts and receive input from others. ChatGPT, can you help us set up a collaborative space for this purpose?

Example Prompt 4:
ChatGPT, we want to host a design sprint where our team can work together to develop a new concept. Can you provide tools and prompts to guide us through the process and keep us on track?

Idea: Design concept documentation

ChatGPT can help in documenting the development process and rationale behind design concepts for future reference.

Example Prompt 1:

Can you assist in creating a detailed design concept documentation for our latest project? We need to outline the development process and rationale behind the design choices made.

Example Prompt 2:

We're looking to create a comprehensive document that explains the design concepts behind our new product. Can you help us articulate the thought process and decision-making involved?

Example Prompt 3:

We need support in documenting the design concepts for our upcoming campaign. Can you help us outline the creative process and reasoning behind our design choices?

Example Prompt 4:

As a graphic designer, I need assistance in creating a detailed design concept documentation for my portfolio. Can you help me articulate the development process and rationale behind my design concepts?

TYPOGRAPHY GUIDANCE

THE ART OF
TYPOGRAPHY: MAKING
WORDS SPEAK

Typography, the art and science of arranging type, is a cornerstone of graphic design. In our AI-infused world, ChatGPT is your trusty companion in mastering the art of typography. Let's dive into the symbiotic relationship between AI and typography with a story about Sarah, a diligent graphic designer.

Sarah is tasked with creating a captivating promotional poster for a tech conference. The challenge? Conveying the event's cutting-edge nature while maintaining readability. Sarah knows that typography is the linchpin here. She turns to ChatGPT for guidance.

"ChatGPT, I need typography that balances innovation and readability," Sarah requests. The AI swiftly responds, "Certainly, Sarah. To convey innovation, consider modern, sans-serif fonts. For readability, prioritize legibility over extravagance. Opt for a larger font size and ample spacing."

With ChatGPT's initial insights, Sarah selects a bold sans-serif font for the poster's headline, ensuring it exudes a contemporary feel. The AI even suggests a complementary serif font for body text, striking a perfect balance.

Next, Sarah needs to pair fonts harmoniously. ChatGPT suggests pairing fonts from the same type family for consistency while varying font weights to create hierarchy. This guidance ensures that her poster is visually appealing and easy to navigate.

But typography is not just about font selection; it's also about layout. Sarah seeks advice on optimizing text placement. ChatGPT recommends employing the grid system for alignment and utilizing AI-powered tools to adjust line spacing and kerning automatically.

As Sarah engages in a dynamic conversation with ChatGPT, she fine-tunes her typographic choices. She experiments with different font pairings, tweaks line heights, and adjusts letter spacing until she achieves a harmonious blend of aesthetics and readability.

With the poster's typography polished to perfection, Sarah's design truly shines. The fonts not only communicate the event's innovation but also ensure that every piece of information is crystal clear. Attendees are captivated by the poster's visual appeal, which draws them in and makes the details effortlessly digestible.

In summary, AI, embodied by ChatGPT, elevates typography from a fundamental skill to an art form. As Sarah's experience illustrates, AI provides actionable advice on font selection, pairing, and layout, ensuring that your designs not only look visually stunning but also convey their message effectively. Embrace AI as your typography guide, and let your designs transcend the ordinary, effortlessly blending aesthetics with functionality.

Task: Font selection

Suggesting appropriate fonts for different design projects

Example Prompt 1:
What type of design project are you working on? Knowing the context will help me suggest the most appropriate fonts for your project.

Example Prompt 2:
Are you looking for a modern and sleek font, or something more traditional and elegant? Understanding the style you're aiming for will guide my font recommendations.

Example Prompt 3:
Do you have any specific brand guidelines or existing fonts that need to be considered in this project? Ensuring consistency with your brand identity is important in font selection.

Example Prompt 4:
Are there any specific emotions or messages you want to convey through your design? Understanding the tone and purpose of your project will help me suggest fonts that align with your goals.

Task: Pairing fonts

Providing recommendations for font combinations that work well together

Example Prompt 1:
Can you suggest a font pairing that would work well for a modern and minimalist website design?

Example Prompt 2:

I'm looking for a font combination that conveys a sense of elegance and sophistication for a luxury brand. Any recommendations?

Example Prompt 3:
What are some font pairings that would complement each other for a playful and whimsical design aesthetic?

Example Prompt 4:
I need a font pairing that balances professionalism with a touch of creativity for a business presentation. Any suggestions?

Task: Font hierarchy

Advising on the use of different font sizes and weights for headings, subheadings, and body text

Example Prompt 1:
Can you provide examples of font hierarchy in a website or publication, including the use of different font sizes and weights for headings, subheadings, and body text?

Example Prompt 2:
How can font hierarchy be used to create visual hierarchy and guide the reader's attention through a design?

Example Prompt 3:
What are some best practices for choosing and pairing fonts for different levels of text in a design, such as headings, subheadings, and body text?

Example Prompt 4:
Can you explain the impact of font hierarchy on readability and user experience, and provide tips for optimizing font choices for different types of content?

Task: Kerning and tracking

Offering guidance on adjusting letter spacing for improved readability and aesthetics

Example Prompt 1:
Can you provide some tips on adjusting kerning and tracking to improve the overall readability and aesthetics of a design?

Example Prompt 2:
How can I effectively adjust letter spacing to create a more visually appealing and balanced layout?

Example Prompt 3:
What are some common mistakes to avoid when adjusting kerning and tracking in graphic design?

Example Prompt 4:
Can you share some examples of how adjusting letter spacing can significantly impact the overall design and readability of a piece?

Task: Line length and spacing

Providing suggestions for optimal line length and line spacing for better readability

Example Prompt 1:
What is the ideal line length and spacing for a paragraph of body text in a printed magazine layout?

Example Prompt 2:
Can you provide examples of websites with effective line length and spacing for easy online reading?

Example Prompt 3:
How can I adjust line length and spacing in my design to accommodate different languages and character sets?

Example Prompt 4:
What are some best practices for line length and spacing in mobile app interfaces to ensure readability on smaller screens?

Task: Font licensing

Assisting in finding and understanding font licensing for commercial use

Example Prompt 1:
Can you provide information on the different types of font licensing available for commercial use, and how to determine which license is needed for a specific project?

Example Prompt 2:
What are the key considerations when selecting a font for commercial use, and how can I ensure that I am properly licensed to use it in my designs?

Example Prompt 3:
Could you explain the process of obtaining a font license for commercial use, including any potential restrictions or limitations that may apply?

Example Prompt 4:
I'm looking for guidance on navigating font licensing for commercial projects. Can you offer tips on where to find reputable sources for licensed fonts and how to ensure compliance with licensing agreements?

Task: Accessibility

Recommending fonts and text treatments that are accessible to all users, including those with visual impairments

Example Prompt 1:
Can you recommend fonts that are easily readable for users with visual impairments, such as sans-serif fonts with clear distinctions between letters?

Example Prompt 2:
What text treatments or styles would you suggest for improving accessibility, particularly for users with color blindness or low vision?

Example Prompt 3:
How can we ensure that our design choices for text and fonts are inclusive and accessible to all users, including those with visual impairments?

Example Prompt 4:
What are some best practices for creating accessible typography and text designs, especially for users who rely on screen readers or other assistive technologies?

Task: Brand consistency

Ensuring that typography choices align with a brand's visual identity and guidelines

Example Prompt 1:
How can we ensure that our typography choices align with our brand's visual identity and guidelines to maintain brand consistency?

Example Prompt 2:
What are some best practices for selecting typography that reflects and reinforces our brand's image and messaging?

Example Prompt 3:
Can you provide examples of how typography can impact brand perception and how we can use it to strengthen our brand identity?

Example Prompt 4:
What tools or resources can we use to create and maintain a cohesive typography system that aligns with our brand's visual identity and guidelines?

Idea: Font Pairing Guide

Create a guide for designers on how to effectively pair different fonts for a cohesive and visually appealing design.

Example Prompt 1:

Can you create a comprehensive font pairing guide for designers, including tips on how to effectively pair different fonts for a cohesive and visually appealing design?

Example Prompt 2:
I need your help in developing a resource for designers that outlines best practices for font pairing to achieve visually appealing designs. Can you assist with this?

Example Prompt 3:
I'm looking to create a guide for designers on how to effectively pair different fonts for a cohesive and visually appealing design. Can you provide support in developing this resource?

Example Prompt 4:
As a graphic designer, I'm in need of a font pairing guide to help me create visually appealing designs. Can you help me develop this resource?

Idea: Typography Cheat Sheet
Develop a cheat sheet with common typography rules and best practices for quick reference.

Example Prompt 1:
Create a visually appealing typography cheat sheet that includes essential rules and best practices for font selection, spacing, and alignment. Use a combination of bold, elegant fonts and eye-catching graphics to make the information easily digestible and memorable.

Example Prompt 2:
Design a typography cheat sheet that showcases the differences between serif and sans-serif fonts, and provides examples of when to use each. Incorporate color-coded sections and clear headings to make the information easy to navigate and understand.

Example Prompt 3:
Develop a typography cheat sheet that includes practical tips for

improving readability, such as line length, leading, and font size. Use a clean, modern layout with plenty of white space to ensure the information is easy to absorb at a glance.

Example Prompt 4:
Produce a typography cheat sheet that highlights common mistakes to avoid, such as improper kerning, inconsistent font pairings, and excessive use of decorative fonts. Incorporate visual examples and clear explanations to help users understand and remember the key principles.

Idea: Brand Typography Guidelines

Assist in creating comprehensive typography guidelines for brands, ensuring consistency across all design materials.

Example Prompt 1:
ChatGPT, I need your help in creating a set of typography guidelines for a new brand. Can you assist in developing a comprehensive set of rules and recommendations for font usage, sizing, and spacing to ensure consistency across all design materials?

Example Prompt 2:
Hey ChatGPT, I'm working on a branding project and need support in establishing typography guidelines. Can you help in outlining the preferred fonts, styles, and hierarchy for the brand's visual identity?

Example Prompt 3:
ChatGPT, I'm looking to create a cohesive visual identity for a brand through typography. Can you provide guidance in developing a set of rules for font pairing, usage, and application across various design assets?

Example Prompt 4:
I'm in need of assistance, ChatGPT, to establish a clear and consistent typography system for a brand. Can you help in defining

the primary and secondary font choices, as well as guidelines for their usage in different design contexts?

Idea: Web Typography Best Practices

Provide tips and tricks for using typography effectively in web design, including responsive typography and accessibility considerations.

Example Prompt 1:

Can you provide a comprehensive guide on web typography best practices, including tips for choosing the right fonts, creating responsive typography, and ensuring accessibility for all users?

Example Prompt 2:

I'm looking for advice on how to effectively use typography in web design, particularly in terms of creating a visually appealing and accessible experience. Can you provide some tips and tricks for achieving this?

Example Prompt 3:

I'm interested in learning more about the best practices for web typography, especially in terms of making it responsive and accessible. Can you share some insights and recommendations for achieving this?

Example Prompt 4:

As a graphic designer, I'm always looking for ways to improve my web typography skills. Can you provide some guidance on using typography effectively in web design, with a focus on responsiveness and accessibility considerations?

Idea: Typography Infographics

Design infographics that visually explain typography concepts and rules for easy understanding.

Example Prompt 1:

Create an infographic that visually explains the concept of kerning and its importance in typography design. Include examples and tips for achieving optimal kerning in different typefaces.

Example Prompt 2:

Design an infographic that breaks down the anatomy of a letter, showcasing the different parts of a typeface and their significance in creating well-balanced typography.

Example Prompt 3:

Develop an infographic that illustrates the various font classifications, such as serif, sans-serif, script, and display, with clear examples and explanations of when to use each type in design.

Example Prompt 4:

Produce an infographic that demystifies typographic hierarchy, demonstrating how to effectively use size, weight, and style variations to create visually appealing and organized typography in design projects.

Idea: Typography Workshops

Host workshops or webinars to educate other designers on the principles of typography and how to apply them in their work.

Example Prompt 1:

Create a promotional poster for an upcoming typography workshop, incorporating various font styles and layout techniques to attract potential attendees.

Example Prompt 2:

Design a series of social media graphics to promote an upcoming webinar on the fundamentals of typography, using engaging visuals and informative text to generate interest.

Example Prompt 3:

Develop a visually appealing presentation template for use during typography workshops, incorporating dynamic typography examples and interactive elements to keep participants engaged.

Example Prompt 4:
Design a digital handout or booklet for workshop attendees, featuring key typography principles, practical tips, and resources to help them apply what they've learned in their own design projects.

Idea: Custom Typography Services

Offer custom typography design services for clients looking for unique and personalized typefaces.

Example Prompt 1:
Create a custom typography design for a luxury fashion brand's logo, incorporating elements of elegance and sophistication.

Example Prompt 2:
Design a personalized typeface for a tech startup's branding, reflecting innovation and modernity in the design.

Example Prompt 3:
Develop a custom typography for a wedding invitation suite, capturing the couple's unique style and personality in the lettering.

Example Prompt 4:
Produce a bespoke typeface for a restaurant's menu and signage, infusing the design with the establishment's distinct ambiance and cuisine.

Idea: Typography Portfolio Showcase

Use ChatGPT to help curate and present a portfolio of typography work, showcasing different styles and applications.

Example Prompt 1:
Create a visually appealing and interactive digital portfolio showcasing a variety of typography styles and applications. Use ChatGPT to help curate and organize the content, ensuring a

seamless and engaging user experience.

Example Prompt 2:
Assist in designing a series of typographic posters, logos, and branding materials to be featured in a comprehensive portfolio. Utilize ChatGPT to gather inspiration, refine design concepts, and ensure consistency across all pieces.

Example Prompt 3:
Collaborate with ChatGPT to develop a dynamic online showcase of typography work, including detailed descriptions of each project, the design process, and the inspiration behind each piece. Ensure the portfolio is visually captivating and easy to navigate.

Example Prompt 4:
Work with ChatGPT to create a visually stunning and cohesive portfolio that highlights the versatility and creativity of typography. Incorporate interactive elements and multimedia content to engage viewers and showcase the breadth of typographic design work.

Idea: Typography Software Tutorials

Create tutorials on using typography software such as Adobe InDesign or Illustrator, covering advanced text manipulation and effects.

Example Prompt 1:
Can you create a step-by-step tutorial on advanced text manipulation in Adobe InDesign, including techniques for creating custom fonts and text effects?

Example Prompt 2:
I'd like to see a tutorial on using typography software like Illustrator to create visually stunning text effects and manipulation. Can you provide a detailed walkthrough on this topic?

Example Prompt 3:

I'm looking for guidance on using Adobe InDesign for advanced typography design. Can you create a tutorial that covers techniques for creating dynamic layouts and text effects?

Example Prompt 4:
I'm interested in learning more about advanced text manipulation in typography software. Can you provide a tutorial on using Illustrator to create custom fonts and intricate text effects?

Idea: Typography Trends Analysis
Use ChatGPT to analyze and report on current typography trends, helping designers stay ahead of the curve.

Example Prompt 1:
Hey ChatGPT, I need your help to analyze and report on current typography trends in the design industry. Can you provide insights on popular font styles, color combinations, and layout techniques that are trending right now?

Example Prompt 2:
ChatGPT, as a graphic designer, I'm looking to stay ahead of the curve with typography trends. Can you analyze and report on the emerging typography styles and design elements that are gaining popularity in the industry?

Example Prompt 3:
I'm curious about the latest typography trends and how they are evolving in the design world. ChatGPT, can you help me analyze and report on the current typography trends, including any innovative techniques or unique font choices that are making waves?

Example Prompt 4:
As a graphic designer, I want to ensure that my typography choices are in line with current trends. ChatGPT, can you provide a comprehensive analysis and report on the latest typography trends, including any notable shifts in design preferences and

emerging styles?

Idea: Typography Booklet Design

Design and produce a booklet on typography guidance, serving as a handy reference for designers.

Example Prompt 1:
Create a visually appealing cover design for a typography booklet, incorporating elements of classic and modern typography styles to capture the essence of the content within.

Example Prompt 2:
Design a series of visually engaging and informative spreads that showcase different typography styles, including serif, sans-serif, script, and decorative fonts, with accompanying explanations and examples.

Example Prompt 3:
Incorporate interactive elements such as QR codes or augmented reality features that allow readers to see live demonstrations of typography usage and applications.

Example Prompt 4:
Produce a visually cohesive layout for the entire booklet, ensuring that the typography, color scheme, and overall design elements complement and enhance the content for a seamless and enjoyable reading experience.

Idea: Typography Consultation Services

Provide one-on-one consultation services for designers seeking advice on typography choices and applications in their projects.

Example Prompt 1:
ChatGPT, I need your help to create a virtual consultation service for designers looking for advice on typography choices. Can you assist in developing a chatbot interface that can provide

one-on-one consultations and recommendations for typography applications in design projects?

Example Prompt 2:

As a graphic designer, I want to offer typography consultation services to other designers. Can you help me create a chatbot that can provide personalized advice and guidance on typography choices and applications in design projects?

Example Prompt 3:

I'm looking to provide specialized typography consultation services to designers. Can you help me develop a chatbot that can offer personalized one-on-one consultations and recommendations for typography choices in design projects?

Example Prompt 4:

I need support in creating a virtual platform for typography consultation services. Can you assist me in developing a chatbot that can provide personalized advice and guidance on typography choices and applications in design projects?

COLOR THEORY
INSIGHTS

SPECTRUM OF EMOTION: MASTERING COLOR THEORY

In the world of graphic design, color theory wields immense power. It's the visual language that speaks directly to emotions, perceptions, and brand identity. In our AI-driven era, ChatGPT emerges as your go-to companion, offering profound insights into the realm of color theory. Let's delve into this partnership through the eyes of Alex, a skilled graphic designer.

Alex is tasked with revamping a restaurant's branding. The objective? Conveying a sense of warmth and inviting ambiance while maintaining a fresh and modern appeal. The secret to achieving this delicate balance lies in mastering color theory. Alex turns to ChatGPT for guidance.

"ChatGPT, I need a color palette that exudes warmth but also feels contemporary," Alex seeks the AI's wisdom. ChatGPT responds promptly, "Certainly, Alex. To evoke warmth, consider warm colors like deep reds, earthy browns, and soft oranges. To maintain a modern touch, balance these with cool neutrals or muted greens and blues."

With ChatGPT's initial guidance, Alex begins experimenting

with color combinations. The AI even suggests using color psychology to tap into the subconscious emotions of potential customers. Warm reds and oranges, for example, evoke feelings of comfort and appetite, which align perfectly with the restaurant's ambiance.

ChatGPT goes a step further, recommending color harmonies like complementary or analogous schemes. Alex realizes the power of these harmonies in creating a visually appealing and emotionally resonant brand identity.

But color theory isn't just about choosing colors; it's also about balance. Alex seeks advice on color proportions. ChatGPT recommends using the 60-30-10 rule: 60% for the dominant color, 30% for the secondary color, and 10% for accents. This formula ensures a harmonious composition that guides the viewer's eye effectively.

As Alex continues the conversation with ChatGPT, the designer fine-tunes the color palette. The AI provides hex codes for precise color selection, making the process seamless. Alex also tests various background and text color combinations to ensure readability and accessibility.

With the revamped branding, the restaurant achieves its goals effortlessly. The color palette not only exudes warmth but also maintains a modern edge, attracting both loyal customers and newcomers. The restaurant's visual identity has become a feast for the eyes and a reflection of its inviting atmosphere.

In conclusion, AI, personified by ChatGPT, brings color theory to life for graphic designers like Alex. It provides invaluable insights into choosing palettes that evoke desired emotions and align with brand identity. As Alex's experience illustrates, AI isn't just a tool; it's a partner in the creative process, ensuring that your designs resonate with audiences on a profound level. Embrace AI's color theory insights, and let your designs speak the language of emotions and brand identity with eloquence and impact.

Task: Color psychology insights

Understanding the emotional and psychological impact of different colors

Example Prompt 1:
Can you explain the emotional associations and psychological effects of using warm colors like red, orange, and yellow in graphic design?

Example Prompt 2:
How do cool colors such as blue, green, and purple influence the mood and perception of a design?

Example Prompt 3:
What are some cultural differences in color symbolism and how can this impact the effectiveness of a design in different regions?

Example Prompt 4:
Can you provide examples of how the use of color in branding and marketing has successfully evoked specific emotions or behaviors in consumers?

Task: Color harmony principles

Exploring complementary, analogous, and triadic color schemes

Example Prompt 1:
Can you explain the concept of complementary colors and how

they create visual harmony in a design?

Example Prompt 2:
What are some examples of analogous color schemes in graphic design, and how do they impact the overall feel of a composition?

Example Prompt 3:
How can the use of triadic color schemes enhance the visual appeal of a design, and what are some best practices for implementing them effectively?

Example Prompt 4:
Discuss the role of color harmony principles in creating a cohesive and balanced color palette for a graphic design project.

Task: Color mixing techniques

Learning about additive and subtractive color mixing

Example Prompt 1:
Can you explain the difference between additive and subtractive color mixing and how they are used in graphic design?

Example Prompt 2:
What are some common color mixing techniques used in graphic design, and how do they impact the final visual outcome?

Example Prompt 3:
How can understanding color theory and mixing techniques enhance the overall impact of a design project?

Example Prompt 4:
Can you provide examples of how additive and subtractive color mixing are used in real-world graphic design projects?

Task: Color contrast and readability

Understanding how to create visually appealing and readable color combinations

Example Prompt 1:
Can you provide some tips on using color contrast to improve readability in graphic design?

Example Prompt 2:
How can I effectively use complementary colors to create visually appealing and readable color combinations?

Example Prompt 3:
What are some best practices for choosing text and background colors to ensure readability in graphic design?

Example Prompt 4:
Can you share some examples of successful designs that effectively use color contrast to enhance readability and visual appeal?

Task: Color symbolism

Researching the cultural and symbolic meanings associated with different colors

Example Prompt 1:
Can you provide a brief overview of the cultural significance of the color red in different societies and historical periods?

Example Prompt 2:
What are some common associations with the color blue in various cultures, and how has its symbolism evolved over time?

Example Prompt 3:
I'm interested in learning about the symbolic meanings of the color yellow in different religious and spiritual traditions. Can you share some insights?

Example Prompt 4:
Could you research and share examples of how the color green has been used symbolically in art, literature, and cultural practices across different regions of the world?

Task: Color trends

Staying updated on current and emerging color trends in design

Example Prompt 1:
What are some of the current popular color trends in graphic design and how can we incorporate them into our projects?

Example Prompt 2:
Can you recommend any resources or tools for staying updated on emerging color trends in design?

Example Prompt 3:
How can we use color psychology to inform our design choices and stay ahead of the curve in terms of color trends?

Example Prompt 4:
What are some examples of successful brands or designs that have effectively utilized current color trends, and how can we apply similar strategies in our own work?

Task: Color perception

Understanding how humans perceive and interpret different colors

Example Prompt 1:
Prompt: "Can you describe a time when you experienced a strong emotional reaction to a specific color? How do you think your personal experiences and cultural background influence your perception of color?"

Example Prompt 2:
Prompt: "Think about a famous painting or artwork that uses color in a powerful way. How do you think the artist's use of color contributes to the overall impact of the piece? What emotions or messages do you think the colors convey?"

Example Prompt 3:
Prompt: *"Consider the concept of color symbolism in different cultures. Can you think of any examples where a specific color holds different meanings or associations in different parts of the world? How does this demonstrate the subjective nature of color perception?"*

Example Prompt 4:
Prompt: *"Reflect on the role of color in branding and marketing. How do companies use color to evoke specific emotions or create a certain image for their products or services? Can you think of any examples where color has played a significant role in a brand's success or failure?"*

Task: Color application in branding

Exploring the use of color in branding and its impact on consumer perception

Example Prompt 1:
How can the strategic use of color in branding influence consumer perception and emotional response to a product or service?

Example Prompt 2:
Discuss the psychological impact of specific colors in branding and how they can evoke different emotions and associations in consumers.

Example Prompt 3:
Explore the role of color harmony and contrast in creating a visually appealing and memorable brand identity.

Example Prompt 4:
Share examples of successful branding campaigns that effectively utilized color to convey a specific message or connect with a target audience.

Task: Color theory in digital design

Applying color theory principles to digital design and user interface (UI) design

Example Prompt 1:
Explain the psychological impact of different colors in digital design and how they can be used to evoke specific emotions or reactions from users.

Example Prompt 2:
Discuss the principles of color harmony and how they can be applied to create visually appealing user interfaces in digital design.

Example Prompt 3:
Provide examples of successful user interface designs that effectively utilize color theory principles to enhance user experience and engagement.

Example Prompt 4:
Explain the importance of contrast, saturation, and brightness in digital design and how they can be used to create hierarchy and visual interest in user interfaces.

Task: Color theory in print design

Applying color theory principles to print materials such as brochures, posters, and packaging

Example Prompt 1:
Explain the psychological impact of different color choices in print design and how they can be used to evoke specific emotions or reactions from the audience.

Example Prompt 2:
Discuss the use of complementary and analogous color schemes in print design and provide examples of how they can be effectively

applied to brochures, posters, and packaging.

Example Prompt 3:
Explore the concept of color harmony in print design and how it can be achieved through the use of color palettes, gradients, and tints to create visually appealing and cohesive print materials.

Example Prompt 4:
Share insights on the importance of considering color contrast and readability in print design, and provide tips for ensuring that text and graphics stand out effectively on printed materials.

Idea: Color psychology in branding

ChatGPT can provide insights on how different colors evoke specific emotions and how they can be used effectively in branding and marketing materials.

Example Prompt 1:
Can you provide insights on how different colors evoke specific emotions and how they can be used effectively in branding and marketing materials? Please include examples of successful brands that have effectively utilized color psychology in their branding.

Example Prompt 2:
I'm looking to understand the impact of color psychology in branding and marketing. Can you provide a breakdown of how different colors can influence consumer behavior and purchasing decisions, and how brands can leverage this knowledge to create effective marketing materials?

Example Prompt 3:
I'm interested in learning more about the role of color psychology in branding and marketing. Can you provide a comprehensive analysis of how different colors can convey specific emotions and how brands can strategically use this knowledge to create a strong brand identity and connect with their target audience?

Example Prompt 4:

I'm curious about the significance of color psychology in branding and marketing. Can you provide insights on how different colors can evoke specific emotions and how brands can use this knowledge to create impactful visual branding and marketing materials that resonate with consumers?

Idea: Color harmony in design

ChatGPT can suggest color combinations and palettes that create a sense of balance and harmony in graphic design projects.

Example Prompt 1:

Hey ChatGPT, as a graphic designer, I'm looking to create a sense of balance and harmony in my latest project. Can you suggest color combinations and palettes that would achieve this effect?

Example Prompt 2:

ChatGPT, I'm working on a new graphic design and I want to ensure that the colors I use create a feeling of harmony. Can you provide me with some color harmony suggestions and palettes to achieve this?

Example Prompt 3:

As a graphic designer, I'm always striving to create designs that exude balance and harmony. Can ChatGPT help me by suggesting color combinations and palettes that would achieve this effect in my latest project?

Example Prompt 4:

ChatGPT, I'm in need of some inspiration for color harmony in my graphic design work. Can you provide me with some suggestions for color combinations and palettes that would help me achieve a sense of balance and harmony in my designs?

Idea: Understanding color temperature

ChatGPT can explain the concept of warm and cool colors

and how they can be used to convey different moods and atmospheres in design.

Example Prompt 1:
Can you explain the difference between warm and cool colors in design and how they can be used to create different emotional responses in viewers?

Example Prompt 2:
Please provide examples of how warm and cool colors have been effectively used in graphic design to convey specific moods or atmospheres.

Example Prompt 3:
How can designers use color temperature to evoke specific emotions or create a certain ambiance in their designs?

Example Prompt 4:
Can you discuss the psychological impact of warm and cool colors in design and how they can influence the way people perceive and interact with visual content?

Idea: Color contrast and accessibility

ChatGPT can provide guidance on choosing colors that have enough contrast for readability and accessibility for all users.

Example Prompt 1:
Hey ChatGPT, as a graphic designer, I need help ensuring that the color contrast in my designs is accessible for all users. Can you provide guidance on choosing colors that have enough contrast for readability and accessibility?

Example Prompt 2:
ChatGPT, I'm working on a project that requires careful consideration of color contrast and accessibility. Can you assist me in selecting colors that are visually appealing while also being accessible to all users?

Example Prompt 3:
As a graphic designer, I want to make sure that my designs are inclusive and accessible to everyone. Can you help me understand how to choose colors with sufficient contrast for readability and accessibility?

Example Prompt 4:
I'm looking to create designs that are not only visually appealing but also accessible to all users. ChatGPT, can you provide guidance on selecting colors with the right contrast for readability and accessibility?

Idea: Color symbolism in different cultures

ChatGPT can offer insights on how colors are interpreted differently in various cultures and how to be mindful of this in global design projects.

Example Prompt 1:
Can you provide examples of how different cultures interpret the color red and its symbolism? How can this understanding be applied to design projects targeting diverse audiences?

Example Prompt 2:
I'm curious about the significance of the color white in various cultures. How can this knowledge be integrated into global design strategies to ensure cultural sensitivity and inclusivity?

Example Prompt 3:
Could you share insights on how the color blue is perceived in different parts of the world? How can this awareness inform design choices for international audiences?

Example Prompt 4:
I'd like to learn more about the cultural meanings associated with the color yellow. How can this knowledge be leveraged to create designs that resonate with diverse cultural perspectives?

Idea: The impact of color on user experience

ChatGPT can discuss how color choices can affect the overall user experience of a design, including readability, navigation, and engagement.

Example Prompt 1:

Prompt: "As a graphic designer, I'm interested in understanding the impact of color on user experience. Can you discuss how different color choices can affect readability, navigation, and engagement in a design?"

Example Prompt 2:

Prompt: "I'm curious about the role of color in user experience. Can you provide insights on how color choices can influence the overall user experience of a design, including its impact on readability, navigation, and engagement?"

Example Prompt 3:

Prompt: "As a graphic designer, I'm exploring the significance of color in user experience. Can you elaborate on how color choices can impact the overall user experience of a design, particularly in terms of readability, navigation, and engagement?"

Example Prompt 4:

Prompt: "I'm seeking to understand the relationship between color and user experience. Can you delve into how color choices can impact the overall user experience of a design, with a focus on readability, navigation, and engagement?"

Idea: Using color to create focal points

ChatGPT can suggest ways to use color to draw attention to specific elements in a design and create focal points.

Example Prompt 1:

How can I use color to create a focal point in a website banner design? Can you suggest color combinations and placement to draw attention to the main message or call-to-action?

Example Prompt 2:
I'm working on a poster for an event and want to make the headline stand out using color. Can you provide suggestions on how to use color to create a focal point and make the text pop?

Example Prompt 3:
I'm designing a product packaging and want to use color to draw attention to the product name and key features. Can you recommend color schemes and techniques to make these elements stand out?

Example Prompt 4:
I'm creating a social media graphic and want to use color to highlight a specific product or promotion. How can I effectively use color to create a focal point and capture the viewer's attention?

Idea: Color trends in design

ChatGPT can provide information on current color trends in the design industry and how to incorporate them into graphic design projects.

Example Prompt 1:
Can you provide insights on the latest color trends in graphic design and how they are being used in different industries?

Example Prompt 2:
I'm looking to incorporate the latest color trends into my graphic design projects. Can you suggest some popular color palettes and how to use them effectively?

Example Prompt 3:
What are some unique ways to incorporate current color trends into graphic design, especially for branding and marketing materials?

Example Prompt 4:

I'd like to stay updated on the ever-changing color trends in design. Can you provide regular updates on new color palettes and how they are being utilized in the design industry?

Idea: Color theory in typography

ChatGPT can explain how color choices can impact the legibility and visual appeal of typography in design.

Example Prompt 1:
Can you provide insights on how different color combinations can affect the readability and visual impact of typography in design?

Example Prompt 2:
How can color theory be applied to typography to enhance the overall design and communication of a message?

Example Prompt 3:
I'm interested in learning more about the psychological effects of color choices in typography and how they can influence the viewer's perception. Can you elaborate on this?

Example Prompt 4:
Could you explain the principles of color contrast and how they can be utilized to improve the legibility and aesthetic appeal of typography in design?

Idea: Color in photography and image editing

ChatGPT can offer tips on using color theory to enhance and manipulate colors in photography and image editing for graphic design projects.

Example Prompt 1:
Hey ChatGPT, can you provide tips on using color theory to enhance the mood and atmosphere of a photograph in image editing for a graphic design project?

Example Prompt 2:

ChatGPT, I need some advice on manipulating colors in a photograph to create a cohesive and visually appealing color scheme for a graphic design project. Can you help with some tips?

Example Prompt 3:
I'm looking to understand how to use color theory to create contrast and balance in a photograph for a graphic design project. Can ChatGPT provide some guidance on this?

Example Prompt 4:
ChatGPT, I'm struggling with color manipulation in image editing for a graphic design project. Can you offer some tips on using color theory to achieve the desired visual impact?

Idea: Color in web design

ChatGPT can provide insights on using color effectively in web design, including considerations for different devices and screen resolutions.

Example Prompt 1:
Can you provide guidance on choosing a color scheme for a responsive web design that looks great on both desktop and mobile devices?

Example Prompt 2:
How can I use color psychology to evoke specific emotions and reactions from users on my website? Can you provide examples and best practices?

Example Prompt 3:
I'm struggling to find the right balance of color contrast for accessibility purposes on my website. Can you offer advice on creating a visually appealing yet accessible color palette?

Example Prompt 4:
What are some innovative ways to incorporate color gradients and overlays in web design to create a modern and dynamic user experience? Can you provide examples and tips for

implementation?

Idea: Creating mood boards
based on color theory

ChatGPT can assist in generating ideas for mood boards that explore different color schemes and their emotional impact for design inspiration.

Example Prompt 1:

ChatGPT, can you help me create a mood board based on complementary color schemes and their emotional impact? I'm looking for design inspiration that evokes harmony and balance.

Example Prompt 2:

I need assistance in generating ideas for a mood board that explores analogous color schemes and their emotional impact. Can ChatGPT help me find design inspiration that conveys warmth and unity?

Example Prompt 3:

ChatGPT, I'm seeking support in creating a mood board that showcases triadic color schemes and their emotional impact. Can you assist me in finding design inspiration that captures vibrancy and contrast?

Example Prompt 4:

I'm looking to create a mood board based on monochromatic color schemes and their emotional impact. Can ChatGPT help me generate ideas for design inspiration that conveys simplicity and elegance?

LAYOUT AND COMPOSITION TECHNIQUES

BALANCING ACT: COMPOSITION AND LAYOUT ESSENTIALS

In the world of graphic design, layout and composition are the architectural blueprints of visual storytelling. It's here that AI, represented by ChatGPT, emerges as a guiding force, offering indispensable insights into crafting balanced and captivating designs. Join us as we journey through the eyes of Emily, a seasoned graphic designer, to explore the harmonious partnership between human creativity and artificial intelligence.

Emily's latest project involves designing a digital magazine spread for a client in the fashion industry. The challenge? To create a layout that seamlessly marries the allure of high-end fashion with readability and user-friendliness. Emily knows that mastering layout and composition is key, and she turns to ChatGPT for guidance.

"ChatGPT, I need a layout that oozes sophistication but also ensures an effortless reading experience," Emily conveys her vision to the AI. ChatGPT responds, "Of course, Emily. To achieve sophistication, consider clean and spacious layouts with a focus on high-quality imagery. For readability, employ a clear hierarchy through font choices, size, and color."

Armed with ChatGPT's initial advice, Emily begins to shape her layout. She selects elegant typefaces that convey the essence of luxury while maintaining legibility. The AI also recommends using a grid system to create structure and alignment, ensuring that elements flow harmoniously across the spread.

As Emily delves deeper into the conversation with ChatGPT, she explores the principles of composition. The AI suggests the rule of thirds to create dynamic and visually pleasing arrangements. It also introduces the concept of the golden ratio to establish proportions that resonate with the human eye.

But it's not just about theory; ChatGPT offers practical tips as well. Emily learns how to use AI-powered tools to adjust image placement, spacing, and alignment with precision, saving her valuable time and effort.

Emily continues to iterate on her design with ChatGPT's guidance, experimenting with different grid layouts, image placements, and text arrangements. The AI provides real-time feedback, helping her strike the perfect balance between sophistication and readability.

In the end, Emily's digital magazine spread is a masterpiece. It exudes sophistication through its clean and spacious design, high-quality imagery, and elegant typography. Simultaneously, it ensures an effortless reading experience, with a clear hierarchy and user-friendly layout.

In conclusion, AI, embodied by ChatGPT, empowers graphic designers like Emily to master the principles of layout and composition. It provides actionable strategies for crafting balanced and engaging designs that captivate audiences while maintaining functionality. As Emily's experience demonstrates, AI isn't just a tool; it's a collaborator in the creative process, elevating the art of design to new heights. Embrace AI's insights, and let your layouts tell compelling visual stories that resonate with impact and sophistication.

Task: Grid systems

ChatGPT can provide information on different types of grid systems and how to effectively use them in layout design.

Example Prompt 1:
Can you explain the differences between a baseline grid and a modular grid system in graphic design, and how each can be effectively utilized in layout design?

Example Prompt 2:
What are some common grid systems used in graphic design, and how can they be adapted to different types of content and design styles?

Example Prompt 3:
How can grid systems help maintain consistency and alignment in layout design, and what are some best practices for implementing them in various design projects?

Example Prompt 4:
Can you provide examples of how grid systems have been used effectively in graphic design, and discuss the impact they have on the overall visual appeal and organization of a layout?

Task: Alignment and spacing

ChatGPT can offer tips and best practices for achieving proper alignment and spacing in design layouts.

Example Prompt 1:

Can you provide some tips for achieving consistent alignment and spacing in design layouts? What are some best practices to ensure a clean and professional look?

Example Prompt 2:

How can I effectively use grids and guides to maintain proper alignment and spacing in my design work? Any recommendations for setting up a grid system for different types of layouts?

Example Prompt 3:

What are some common mistakes to avoid when it comes to alignment and spacing in design? How can I troubleshoot and fix issues with uneven spacing or misaligned elements?

Example Prompt 4:

I'm struggling with achieving balanced and harmonious spacing in my design compositions. Can you suggest some techniques or tools to help me improve my alignment and spacing skills?

Task: Visual hierarchy

ChatGPT can suggest techniques for creating visual hierarchy in layouts to guide the viewer's attention.

Example Prompt 1:

How can I use contrast in color, size, and shape to create visual hierarchy in my design?

Example Prompt 2:

What are some techniques for using typography to establish a clear visual hierarchy in a layout?

Example Prompt 3:

Can you suggest ways to use spacing and alignment to direct the viewer's attention in a design?

Example Prompt 4:
What are some best practices for organizing and prioritizing information to create a strong visual hierarchy in a layout?

Task: Typography

ChatGPT can provide insights on choosing and pairing typefaces, as well as tips for effective typography in layout design.

Example Prompt 1:
Can you provide examples of typefaces that work well together in a modern layout design?

Example Prompt 2:
What are some tips for creating hierarchy and emphasis with typography in a chat interface?

Example Prompt 3:
How can I effectively use contrast and scale in typography to improve readability in my design?

Example Prompt 4:
Can you suggest typefaces that convey a sense of professionalism and trustworthiness for a business chat interface?

Task: Color theory

ChatGPT can explain color theory principles and how to apply them in layout and composition for effective visual communication.

Example Prompt 1:
Can you explain the principles of color theory and how they can be applied to create visually appealing layouts and compositions?

Example Prompt 2:

How can different color combinations evoke different emotions or convey different messages in visual communication?

Example Prompt 3:
What are some best practices for using color theory to create a cohesive and harmonious color palette in graphic design?

Example Prompt 4:
Can you provide examples of how color theory can be used to create emphasis and hierarchy in visual compositions?

Task: Balance and proportion

ChatGPT can offer advice on achieving balance and proportion in layout design to create visually appealing compositions.

Example Prompt 1:
How can I use different visual elements such as size, color, and spacing to create a balanced and proportionate layout design?

Example Prompt 2:
What are some techniques for achieving visual balance and proportion in a design without making it feel too symmetrical or predictable?

Example Prompt 3:
Can ChatGPT suggest ways to create a sense of harmony and equilibrium in my layout design while still maintaining visual interest?

Example Prompt 4:
I'm struggling with achieving balance and proportion in my design. Can ChatGPT provide tips for effectively using negative space and alignment to create a cohesive composition?

Task: Image placement and cropping

ChatGPT can provide guidance on effective image placement and cropping techniques for layout design.

Example Prompt 1:
Can you provide tips on how to effectively place images within a design layout to create a visually appealing composition?

Example Prompt 2:
What are some best practices for cropping images to maintain focus on the subject while fitting within a specific design layout?

Example Prompt 3:
How can I use image placement to create a sense of balance and flow within a design?

Example Prompt 4:
Can you suggest techniques for integrating text with images in a way that enhances the overall layout design?

Task: Use of white space

ChatGPT can suggest ways to effectively utilize white space in layouts for improved visual impact and readability.

Example Prompt 1:
How can I use white space to create a clean and modern look in my graphic design layout?

Example Prompt 2:
Can you suggest ways to incorporate white space to improve the readability of my design?

Example Prompt 3:
I'm struggling to find the right balance of white space in my layout, can you provide some tips or examples to help me?

Example Prompt 4:
What are some creative ways to use white space to draw attention to key elements in my design?

Idea: Grid Systems

ChatGPT can provide information on different types of grid systems and how to effectively use them in layout design.

Example Prompt 1:
Can you provide an overview of the different types of grid systems used in graphic design, and how they can be applied to create effective layout designs?

Example Prompt 2:
I'm looking to understand the principles behind grid systems in graphic design. Can you explain how to effectively use them to create visually appealing layouts?

Example Prompt 3:
I'm interested in learning more about grid systems and how they can improve the organization and structure of my design work. Can you provide guidance on implementing grid systems effectively?

Example Prompt 4:
I'd like to explore the concept of grid systems in graphic design and how they can enhance the overall composition of a design. Can you share insights on best practices for utilizing grid systems in layout design?

Idea: Visual Hierarchy

ChatGPT can suggest techniques for creating visual hierarchy through size, color, and placement of elements.

Example Prompt 1:
As a Graphic Designer, I need ChatGPT to suggest techniques for creating visual hierarchy through size, color, and placement of elements in a website design I'm working on. Can you provide some tips and best practices for achieving effective visual hierarchy?

Example Prompt 2:
I'm working on a new branding project and I'd like ChatGPT to help me understand how to use size, color, and placement of elements

to create a strong visual hierarchy in my designs. Can you provide some examples and suggestions for achieving this?

Example Prompt 3:
ChatGPT, as a Graphic Designer, I'm looking for guidance on how to effectively use size, color, and placement of elements to establish visual hierarchy in my print designs. Can you offer some advice and techniques for achieving this?

Example Prompt 4:
I'm designing a new infographic and I'd like ChatGPT to assist me in understanding how to use size, color, and placement of elements to create a clear visual hierarchy. Can you provide some insights and recommendations for achieving this in my design?

Idea: Balance and Symmetry

ChatGPT can provide tips on achieving balance and symmetry in layout design to create a visually appealing composition.

Example Prompt 1:
Hey ChatGPT, can you provide tips on how to achieve balance and symmetry in graphic design layouts? I'm looking to create visually appealing compositions and could use some guidance.

Example Prompt 2:
ChatGPT, I'm working on a design project and I want to ensure it has a sense of balance and symmetry. Can you help me understand how to achieve this in my layout?

Example Prompt 3:
I'm struggling to create a visually appealing composition with balance and symmetry in my graphic design. ChatGPT, can you provide some tips or examples to help me improve?

Example Prompt 4:
As a graphic designer, I'm always looking to enhance the balance and symmetry in my layouts. ChatGPT, can you share some best practices or techniques to achieve this in my designs?

Idea: Rule of Thirds

ChatGPT can explain the rule of thirds and how it can be used to create dynamic and balanced layouts.

Example Prompt 1:

Can you provide a brief explanation of the rule of thirds and how it can be applied to graphic design to create visually appealing layouts?

Example Prompt 2:

How can the rule of thirds be used to guide the placement of elements in a design to achieve balance and visual interest?

Example Prompt 3:

I'd like to understand how the rule of thirds can be utilized in graphic design to create dynamic and engaging compositions. Can you provide some examples and explanations?

Example Prompt 4:

Could you walk me through the process of using the rule of thirds to create a balanced and visually appealing layout in graphic design? I'd love to understand the practical application of this concept.

Idea: Typography Pairing

ChatGPT can suggest techniques for pairing different typefaces to create harmonious and visually interesting layouts.

Example Prompt 1:

As a Graphic Designer, I'm looking for suggestions on how to pair a bold, modern sans-serif typeface with a more traditional serif font for a sleek and sophisticated look. Can ChatGPT provide techniques for achieving this typography pairing?

Example Prompt 2:

I'm working on a project that requires pairing a decorative script font with a clean and minimalistic sans-serif typeface. Can ChatGPT offer advice on how to balance these contrasting styles for a visually appealing design?

Example Prompt 3:
I'm interested in creating a typography pairing that combines a vintage-inspired display font with a contemporary geometric typeface. Can ChatGPT provide insights on how to achieve a cohesive and balanced composition with these contrasting styles?

Example Prompt 4:
I'm looking to experiment with pairing a hand-drawn, whimsical typeface with a sleek and modern slab serif font. Can ChatGPT suggest techniques for creating a harmonious and visually interesting typography pairing with these contrasting styles?

Idea: White Space

ChatGPT can provide guidance on using white space effectively to improve the overall composition of a design.

Example Prompt 1:
Hey ChatGPT, as a graphic designer, I'm looking for some guidance on using white space effectively in my designs. Can you provide some tips on how to create a balanced composition using white space?

Example Prompt 2:
ChatGPT, I'm working on a new project and I want to make sure I'm using white space in a way that enhances the overall design. Can you help me understand how to strategically incorporate white space for maximum impact?

Example Prompt 3:
As a graphic designer, I know the importance of white space in design, but I could use some fresh ideas. Can ChatGPT suggest some innovative ways to use white space to create a more visually appealing composition?

Example Prompt 4:

I'm struggling to find the right balance of white space in my designs. ChatGPT, can you provide some examples or case studies of how white space has been effectively used in graphic design to elevate the overall aesthetic?

Idea: Alignment

ChatGPT can offer tips on achieving proper alignment of elements to create a cohesive and organized layout.

Example Prompt 1:

Hey ChatGPT, as a graphic designer, I'm looking for tips on achieving proper alignment of elements in my designs. Can you provide some guidance on creating a cohesive and organized layout?

Example Prompt 2:

ChatGPT, I'm working on a new project and I want to ensure that my design has proper alignment of elements. Can you offer some advice on how to achieve this for a more polished look?

Example Prompt 3:

As a graphic designer, I often struggle with achieving the right alignment of elements in my designs. Can ChatGPT provide some practical tips and techniques for creating a well-organized layout?

Example Prompt 4:

I'm in the process of designing a new website and I want to make sure that all the elements are properly aligned. Can ChatGPT assist me with some best practices for achieving proper alignment in my design?

Idea: Contrast

ChatGPT can explain the importance of contrast in layout design and provide suggestions for creating contrast through color, size, and shape.

Example Prompt 1:
Hey ChatGPT, as a graphic designer, I'm looking to understand the importance of contrast in layout design. Can you explain the significance of contrast and provide suggestions for creating contrast through color, size, and shape in design layouts?

Example Prompt 2:
ChatGPT, I need some guidance on creating impactful contrast in my design work. Can you provide tips on using color, size, and shape to achieve effective contrast in layout design?

Example Prompt 3:
As a graphic designer, I'm interested in learning more about the role of contrast in layout design. Can you explain how contrast can enhance visual appeal and provide examples of how to effectively utilize contrast in design?

Example Prompt 4:
ChatGPT, I'm seeking advice on incorporating contrast into my design layouts. Can you share insights on the importance of contrast and offer practical suggestions for using color, size, and shape to create visually striking contrasts in design?

Idea: Repetition

ChatGPT can suggest ways to use repetition of elements to create a sense of unity and cohesiveness in a layout.

Example Prompt 1:
As a graphic designer, I need ideas on how to effectively use repetition of elements to create a cohesive and unified layout. Can ChatGPT suggest different ways to incorporate repetition in design to achieve this goal?

Example Prompt 2:
I'm looking for inspiration on how to use repetition in my graphic design projects to establish a sense of unity and coherence. Can ChatGPT provide examples and techniques for effectively

implementing repetition in layouts?

Example Prompt 3:
How can repetition be utilized in graphic design to bring harmony and consistency to a composition? Can ChatGPT offer suggestions and tips for using repetition to create a cohesive visual experience?

Example Prompt 4:
I'm seeking guidance on how to leverage the power of repetition in graphic design to achieve a unified and harmonious layout. Can ChatGPT provide insights and best practices for incorporating repetition in design projects?

Idea: Visual Flow

ChatGPT can provide advice on creating a visual flow within a layout to guide the viewer's eye through the design.

Example Prompt 1:
Hey ChatGPT, as a graphic designer, I'm looking to create a visual flow within a website homepage. Can you provide advice on how to guide the viewer's eye through the design and create a seamless visual journey?

Example Prompt 2:
ChatGPT, I'm working on a magazine layout and I want to ensure there's a strong visual flow from one page to the next. Can you offer tips on creating a cohesive visual journey for the reader?

Example Prompt 3:
As a graphic designer, I'm tasked with designing a poster for an event. I want to make sure the design has a clear visual flow to draw the viewer's attention. Can you provide guidance on how to achieve this?

Example Prompt 4:
ChatGPT, I'm working on a product packaging design and I want to ensure there's a smooth visual flow that leads the customer's eye to key information and imagery. Can you offer advice on creating an

effective visual journey within the packaging design?

Idea: Focal Point

ChatGPT can offer techniques for creating a strong focal point within a layout to draw the viewer's attention.

Example Prompt 1:

Hey ChatGPT, as a graphic designer, I'm looking for techniques to create a strong focal point within a layout. Can you provide some tips and tricks to help draw the viewer's attention to the most important element of the design?

Example Prompt 2:

ChatGPT, I'm working on a new project and I want to make sure I create a strong focal point within the layout. Can you suggest some design principles or examples that can help me achieve this?

Example Prompt 3:

As a graphic designer, I often struggle with creating a focal point within my designs. Can ChatGPT provide some guidance on how to use color, contrast, and composition to make the most important element stand out?

Example Prompt 4:

I'm working on a new graphic design project and I want to ensure that I create a strong focal point to capture the viewer's attention. Can ChatGPT offer some advice on how to achieve this through typography, imagery, and layout?

Idea: Rule of Odds

ChatGPT can explain the rule of odds and how it can be used to create visually appealing and balanced compositions.

Example Prompt 1:

Can you provide examples of how the rule of odds is used in graphic design to create visually appealing compositions?

Example Prompt 2:

Please explain how the rule of odds can be applied to photography and graphic design to create balanced and engaging visuals.

Example Prompt 3:

How can the rule of odds be used to create a sense of harmony and balance in a graphic design layout?

Example Prompt 4:

I'd like to understand how the rule of odds can be utilized in typography and iconography to enhance visual appeal. Can you provide some insights?

BRAND IDENTITY DEVELOPMENT

CRAFTING IDENTITIES: THE ART OF BRAND CREATION

In the ever-evolving landscape of graphic design, crafting a cohesive brand identity is both an art and a science. Today, we explore the fusion of creativity and artificial intelligence, exemplified by ChatGPT, in the realm of brand identity development. Join us as we follow the journey of Mark, a graphic designer on a mission to create a captivating brand identity for a start-up in the tech industry.

Mark's client, a forward-thinking tech start-up, seeks a brand identity that encapsulates innovation, trustworthiness, and accessibility. The challenge? To distill these abstract concepts into a visual language that resonates with the target audience. Mark turns to ChatGPT for invaluable insights.

"ChatGPT, I need to develop a brand identity that exudes innovation and trustworthiness while remaining approachable," Mark articulates his client's vision. ChatGPT responds with authority, "Certainly, Mark. To convey innovation, consider modern, forward-looking design elements. For trustworthiness, opt for clean and professional aesthetics. To maintain approachability, infuse friendly colors and shapes."

With ChatGPT's initial guidance, Mark embarks on a creative journey. He explores cutting-edge design trends, incorporating sleek lines, futuristic shapes, and a minimalist approach to convey innovation. To evoke trustworthiness, he selects a clean and professional typeface for the logo and branding materials.

Mark also dives into color theory, seeking to strike the perfect balance between innovation and approachability. ChatGPT recommends a color palette that includes vibrant blues for trustworthiness, coupled with a pop of energetic orange to signify innovation. The AI even suggests using color psychology to create an emotional connection with the audience.

But it's not just about visuals; it's about narrative. Mark seeks advice on crafting a compelling brand story. ChatGPT encourages him to use AI-driven natural language generation to create a brand narrative that aligns with the visual identity. This ensures that the brand message is consistent across all touchpoints.

As Mark continues his collaboration with ChatGPT, he fine-tunes the brand identity, iterates on the logo, and refines the typography choices. The AI's real-time feedback and suggestions prove invaluable, allowing him to confidently present a cohesive brand identity to the client.

In the end, Mark's brand identity captivates the start-up's target audience. It embodies innovation with its sleek design elements, instills trustworthiness through its professional aesthetics, and maintains approachability with its friendly color palette. The brand narrative, seamlessly generated with AI assistance, resonates with authenticity and clarity.

In conclusion, the synergy of human creativity and AI, exemplified by ChatGPT, empowers graphic designers like Mark to craft cohesive brand identities that speak volumes. It offers actionable strategies for developing logos, color schemes, typography, and brand narratives that align with brand values and appeal to the target audience. As Mark's journey illustrates, AI isn't just a tool; it's a partner in the creative process, ensuring that brand identities resonate with authenticity and impact. Embrace AI in your brand identity development, and watch your designs become the visual embodiment of your client's vision and values.

Note: This chapter highlights the utility of AI in generating images that enhance the understanding of strategies, tasks, and ideas. For detailed information, refer to my video training on: jeroenerne.com/AI-images

Task: Market research

Gathering information on target audience, competitors, and industry trends

Example Prompt 1:
What are the key demographics and psychographics of our target audience? How can we effectively reach and engage with them through visual design?

Example Prompt 2:
What are the current design trends in our industry and how can we incorporate them into our marketing materials to stay

competitive?

Example Prompt 3:

Who are our main competitors and what visual strategies are they using to appeal to our shared target audience? How can we differentiate our design approach?

Example Prompt 4:

What are the emerging technologies and platforms that our target audience is using, and how can we adapt our graphic design to effectively communicate with them on these platforms?

Task: Mood board creation

Compiling visual inspiration and references for the brand's aesthetic

Example Prompt 1:

Create a mood board that captures the essence of our brand's aesthetic, incorporating elements such as color palettes, typography, and imagery that reflect our brand identity.

Example Prompt 2:

Compile visual references that evoke the mood and tone we want to convey through our brand, including images, textures, and patterns that align with our desired aesthetic.

Example Prompt 3:

Design a mood board that showcases the visual inspiration behind our brand, highlighting key elements such as mood, style, and overall vibe that we want to communicate to our audience.

Example Prompt 4:

Curate a collection of images, graphics, and design elements that encapsulate the visual direction we want to take for our brand, reflecting our desired aesthetic and brand personality.

Task: Logo design

Creating a unique and memorable visual representation of the brand

Example Prompt 1:
Design a logo that captures the essence of our brand's identity and values, while also being visually striking and memorable.

Example Prompt 2:
Create a logo that effectively communicates our brand's story and mission, while also being versatile enough to work across various platforms and applications.

Example Prompt 3:
Develop a logo that sets us apart from our competitors and leaves a lasting impression on our target audience, while also being timeless and adaptable to future brand developments.

Example Prompt 4:
Produce a logo that embodies the personality and character of our brand, while also being scalable and easily recognizable in both digital and print formats.

Task: Color palette selection

Choosing a cohesive and impactful set of colors for the brand

Example Prompt 1:
Create a color palette that reflects the brand's values and personality, while also considering the psychological impact of each color on the audience.

Example Prompt 2:
Consider the brand's target audience and their preferences when selecting a color palette that resonates with them.

Example Prompt 3:
Explore different color combinations and their potential impact on brand recognition and memorability.

Example Prompt 4:

Incorporate the brand's existing visual elements, such as logo and typography, into the color palette to ensure a cohesive and harmonious overall brand identity.

Task: Typography selection

Identifying and pairing fonts that reflect the brand's personality

Example Prompt 1:
Can you suggest a font that conveys a modern and sleek aesthetic for a tech startup's branding materials?

Example Prompt 2:
What font pairing would best represent a luxury fashion brand with a sophisticated and elegant personality?

Example Prompt 3:
I'm looking for a font that exudes a sense of playfulness and creativity for a children's toy company. Any recommendations?

Example Prompt 4:
How can I find a font combination that reflects a vintage and nostalgic vibe for a retro-themed restaurant's menu design?

Task: Brand guidelines creation

Establishing rules and standards for the brand's visual identity

Example Prompt 1:
Can you provide examples of previous brand designs and logos to help establish a visual direction for the brand guidelines?

Example Prompt 2:
What are the key colors and typography that should be consistently used across all brand materials?

Example Prompt 3:
How should the brand's imagery and photography style be represented in the brand guidelines?

Example Prompt 4:
What are the dos and don'ts when it comes to using the brand's logo and other visual elements in different marketing materials?

Task: Collateral design

Developing various branded materials such as business cards, letterheads, and packaging

Example Prompt 1:
Create a visually appealing business card design that incorporates our brand colors and logo, while also including essential contact information in a clear and professional manner.

Example Prompt 2:
Design a letterhead template that reflects our brand identity and can be easily customized for different departments or individuals within the company.

Example Prompt 3:
Develop packaging designs for our new product line that not only showcases the product effectively but also communicates our brand message and values to the consumer.

Example Prompt 4:
Produce a set of branded materials, including business cards, letterheads, and packaging, that maintain a cohesive visual identity across all touchpoints and effectively represent our brand in the market.

Task: Brand messaging

Crafting the language and tone that represents the brand's values and mission

Example Prompt 1:
How can we visually communicate our brand's commitment to sustainability and environmental responsibility through our

design choices and messaging?

Example Prompt 2:
What language and tone best align with our brand's mission of inclusivity and diversity, and how can we incorporate these values into our visual branding?

Example Prompt 3:
In what ways can we use graphic design to convey our brand's dedication to innovation and forward-thinking, while maintaining a relatable and approachable tone?

Example Prompt 4:
How can we ensure that our brand messaging and visual design effectively convey our commitment to quality and excellence, while also resonating with our target audience?

Task: Visual style development

Defining the overall look and feel of the brand across different platforms

Example Prompt 1:
Create a series of mood boards that capture the essence of our brand, incorporating color palettes, typography, and imagery that reflect our desired visual style.

Example Prompt 2:
Design a set of social media templates that maintain a cohesive look and feel across various platforms, while also allowing for flexibility and creativity in content creation.

Example Prompt 3:
Develop a style guide that outlines the specific design elements, such as logo usage, iconography, and layout principles, to ensure consistency in our brand's visual representation.

Example Prompt 4:
Produce a series of mockups for our website and mobile

app, showcasing how the visual style translates across different digital platforms and devices, while maintaining a seamless user experience.

Task: Brand asset management

Organizing and maintaining the brand's visual elements for consistency

Example Prompt 1:

How can we create a system for organizing and categorizing our brand's visual elements to ensure easy access and consistency across all marketing materials?

Example Prompt 2:

What are some best practices for maintaining a library of brand assets, such as logos, color palettes, and typography, to ensure they are always up-to-date and easily accessible for design projects?

Example Prompt 3:

Can you provide tips for creating a style guide that effectively communicates the usage and guidelines for our brand's visual elements, ensuring consistency across all platforms and materials?

Example Prompt 4:

What tools or software do you recommend for efficiently managing and organizing our brand's visual assets, and how can we integrate them into our design workflow for maximum effectiveness?

Idea: Logo Design

ChatGPT can help generate ideas for unique and memorable logo designs that represent the brand's identity.

Example Prompt 1:

Can you help me brainstorm some creative concepts for a logo design that captures the essence of our brand's identity and values?

Example Prompt 2:

I'm looking for inspiration for a logo that will stand out and make a lasting impression. Can you assist with generating some innovative ideas?

Example Prompt 3:

I need assistance in coming up with a visually striking and meaningful logo design. Can you provide some suggestions to spark my creativity?

Example Prompt 4:

I'm seeking support in developing a logo that effectively communicates our brand's story and personality. Can you help generate some fresh and original concepts?

Idea: Color Palette Selection

ChatGPT can suggest color combinations that evoke the desired emotions and align with the brand's personality.

Example Prompt 1:

Hey ChatGPT, as a graphic designer, I need help with color palette selection for a new brand. Can you suggest color combinations that evoke a sense of trustworthiness and professionalism, while still feeling modern and approachable?

Example Prompt 2:

ChatGPT, I'm working on a project for a wellness brand and I need help with color palette selection. Can you suggest combinations that convey a feeling of calm and relaxation, while still maintaining a sense of energy and vitality?

Example Prompt 3:

As a graphic designer, I'm looking for color palette suggestions for a tech startup. Can ChatGPT help me find combinations that exude innovation and forward-thinking, while also feeling sleek and sophisticated?

Example Prompt 4:

ChatGPT, I'm designing for a fashion brand and I need help with color palette selection. Can you suggest combinations that capture a sense of luxury and elegance, while still feeling vibrant and trend-setting?

Idea: Typography Selection

ChatGPT can provide recommendations for fonts that reflect the brand's tone and style.

Example Prompt 1:

Hey ChatGPT, I'm working on a new branding project and I need some help with typography selection. Can you recommend some fonts that convey a modern and sleek vibe for a tech startup?

Example Prompt 2:

Hi there, ChatGPT! I'm designing a logo for a luxury fashion brand and I'm struggling to find the perfect font. Can you suggest some elegant and sophisticated typefaces that would complement the brand's image?

Example Prompt 3:

Hey ChatGPT, I'm revamping the website for a playful and fun children's toy company. Can you provide me with some font recommendations that capture the brand's whimsical and energetic personality?

Example Prompt 4:

Hello ChatGPT, I'm working on a rebranding project for a classic and timeless heritage company. I need help finding fonts that exude tradition and sophistication. Can you assist me with some suitable typeface options?

Idea: Brand Style Guide Creation

ChatGPT can assist in creating a comprehensive style guide that outlines the brand's visual identity, including logo usage, color codes, and typography guidelines.

Example Prompt 1:

Hey ChatGPT, I need your help in creating a brand style guide for a new company. Can you assist in outlining the logo usage, color codes, and typography guidelines to ensure a cohesive visual identity?

Example Prompt 2:
ChatGPT, I'm looking to establish a consistent visual identity for a brand. Can you support in developing a comprehensive style guide that includes logo usage, color codes, and typography guidelines?

Example Prompt 3:
I'm in need of a brand style guide for a client's new business. Can ChatGPT help in creating a detailed document that outlines the visual identity, including logo usage, color codes, and typography guidelines?

Example Prompt 4:
ChatGPT, I'm working on a project that requires a brand style guide. Can you assist in developing a comprehensive document that outlines the brand's visual identity, including logo usage, color codes, and typography guidelines?

Idea: Brand Storytelling

ChatGPT can help craft compelling narratives and messaging that communicate the brand's values and mission.

Example Prompt 1:
Create a brand storytelling narrative for a sustainable fashion brand that emphasizes the importance of ethical production and environmental responsibility.

Example Prompt 2:
Develop a compelling brand story for a tech startup that focuses on innovation and disrupting the industry with cutting-edge solutions.

Example Prompt 3:
Craft a narrative for a wellness brand that promotes holistic

health and self-care, emphasizing the importance of mental and physical well-being.

Example Prompt 4:
Help create a brand storytelling strategy for a social impact organization that aims to make a difference in the community through advocacy and empowerment.

Idea: Packaging Design

ChatGPT can offer ideas for packaging designs that align with the brand's identity and appeal to the target audience.

Example Prompt 1:
Create a packaging design concept for a luxury skincare brand targeting young professionals in urban areas. Consider using sleek, minimalist elements and a color palette that exudes sophistication and modernity.

Example Prompt 2:
Develop a packaging design for a line of eco-friendly household cleaning products that appeals to environmentally conscious consumers. Incorporate natural textures and earthy tones to convey sustainability and purity.

Example Prompt 3:
Design packaging for a new line of artisanal chocolates aimed at a high-end market. Utilize elegant typography and rich, indulgent colors to evoke a sense of luxury and decadence.

Example Prompt 4:
Brainstorm packaging ideas for a line of children's toys that are vibrant, playful, and whimsical. Incorporate fun illustrations and interactive elements to engage young consumers and their parents.

Idea: Stationery Design

ChatGPT can provide inspiration for business cards, letterheads, and other stationery items that reflect the brand's visual identity.

Example Prompt 1:
Prompt: "ChatGPT, can you help me brainstorm ideas for a modern and sleek business card design that incorporates our company logo and color scheme?"

Example Prompt 2:
Prompt: "I'm looking for inspiration for a professional letterhead design that captures the essence of our brand. Can ChatGPT suggest some creative concepts?"

Example Prompt 3:
Prompt: "I need assistance in creating a cohesive stationery design that reflects our brand's visual identity. Can ChatGPT provide ideas for business cards, letterheads, and other stationery items that convey our brand message?"

Example Prompt 4:
Prompt: "ChatGPT, can you assist me in developing a unique and eye-catching stationery design that aligns with our brand's aesthetic and values?"

Idea: Brand Collateral Design

ChatGPT can assist in creating various branded materials such as brochures, flyers, and posters that maintain consistency with the brand's identity.

Example Prompt 1:
Prompt: "Hey ChatGPT, I need your help in designing a series of brochures for our upcoming product launch. Can you assist in creating visually appealing and consistent branded materials that align with our brand's identity?"

Example Prompt 2:
Prompt: "ChatGPT, I'm looking to revamp our company's flyer designs to better reflect our brand's image. Can you support in creating eye-catching and cohesive branded materials that will

grab the attention of our target audience?"

Example Prompt 3:

Prompt: "I'm in need of some new posters for our upcoming event, and I want them to be in line with our brand's identity. ChatGPT, can you help in designing visually striking and on-brand posters that will effectively promote our event?"

Example Prompt 4:

Prompt: "ChatGPT, I'm working on creating a set of branded materials for our marketing campaign, including brochures, flyers, and posters. Can you assist in ensuring that all these materials maintain consistency with our brand's identity and effectively communicate our message to our audience?"

Idea: Website Design

ChatGPT can offer suggestions for website layouts and visual elements that reinforce the brand's identity and enhance user experience.

Example Prompt 1:

Hey ChatGPT, as a graphic designer, I'm looking for some fresh ideas for a website layout that will really make our brand stand out. Can you suggest some unique visual elements and design concepts that will enhance the user experience and reinforce our brand identity?

Example Prompt 2:

ChatGPT, I need some help with website design. Can you provide suggestions for creating a visually appealing layout that aligns with our brand's identity and improves user engagement? I'm looking for ideas to make our website more interactive and user-friendly.

Example Prompt 3:

As a graphic designer, I'm seeking inspiration for website design that will elevate our brand's online presence. Can ChatGPT offer suggestions for incorporating visual elements and layout ideas that will enhance the user experience and effectively communicate our brand's identity?

Example Prompt 4:

ChatGPT, I'm working on a website design project and I need some creative input. Can you provide recommendations for visual elements and layout ideas that will help reinforce our brand's identity and create a more engaging user experience? I'm looking for fresh ideas to make our website design really stand out.

Idea: Social Media Graphics

ChatGPT can help generate ideas for social media posts and graphics that align with the brand's visual identity and messaging.

Example Prompt 1:

Prompt: "Hey ChatGPT, I need some fresh ideas for social media graphics that reflect our brand's visual identity and messaging. Can you help brainstorm some concepts that will resonate with our audience and stand out on our social media platforms?"

Example Prompt 2:

Prompt: "ChatGPT, I'm looking for some creative inspiration for our social media posts and graphics. Can you assist in generating ideas that align with our brand's visual identity and messaging, while also capturing the attention of our followers?"

Example Prompt 3:

Prompt: "As a graphic designer, I'm seeking ChatGPT's support in developing social media graphics that effectively communicate our brand's visual identity and messaging. Can you provide suggestions for engaging and visually appealing content that will enhance our online presence?"

Example Prompt 4:

Prompt: "ChatGPT, I need assistance in creating social media graphics that are in line with our brand's visual identity and messaging. Can you help generate ideas for posts and graphics that will help us connect with our audience and convey our brand's message effectively?"

Idea: Brand Merchandise Design

ChatGPT can provide concepts for branded merchandise such as apparel, accessories, and promotional items that resonate with the brand's identity.

Example Prompt 1:
Prompt: As a Graphic Designer, I need ChatGPT to provide concepts for branded merchandise design for a new clothing line. The brand's identity is centered around sustainability and minimalism, so I need ideas for eco-friendly apparel and accessories that reflect these values.

Example Prompt 2:
Prompt: I'm working on a promotional campaign for a tech company and need ChatGPT to help generate concepts for branded merchandise design. The brand's identity is modern and innovative, so I'm looking for ideas for tech accessories and promotional items that align with this image.

Example Prompt 3:
Prompt: As a Graphic Designer, I'm tasked with creating branded merchandise for a music festival. I need ChatGPT to assist in generating concepts for apparel and accessories that capture the festival's vibrant and energetic atmosphere, while also reflecting the brand's identity.

Example Prompt 4:
Prompt: I'm working with a sports team to develop branded merchandise for their fan base. I need ChatGPT to provide concepts for apparel and accessories that embody the team's spirit and identity, while also appealing to their diverse fan base.

Idea: Brand Voice Development

ChatGPT can assist in defining the brand's tone of voice and language style to ensure consistency across all communication channels.

Example Prompt 1:

Create a brand voice development guide for our company, outlining the tone of voice and language style to be used in all communication materials. Consider our target audience and brand personality in the development process.

Example Prompt 2:

Generate a set of sample social media posts and marketing copy that align with our brand's tone of voice and language style. Ensure the content reflects our brand values and resonates with our audience.

Example Prompt 3:

Assist in crafting a brand messaging framework that encompasses our brand's tone of voice and language style. This should serve as a reference for all internal and external communication to maintain consistency.

Example Prompt 4:

Help in creating a brand style guide that includes guidelines for our brand's tone of voice and language style. This should cover everything from website copy to customer service interactions, ensuring a cohesive brand voice across all touchpoints.

FEEDBACK INTERPRETATION AND REFINEMENT

REVISIONS AND REVELATIONS: REFINING DESIGN CONCEPTS

In the intricate dance of graphic design, client feedback is the compass that guides us to the destination of a successful project. This chapter explores how AI, embodied by ChatGPT, can transform the way designers interpret feedback and refine their creations. Let's follow the journey of Rachel, an experienced graphic designer, as she navigates the art of feedback interpretation and refinement.

Rachel is in the midst of a project for a client launching a new wellness app. She's created a set of app screens that she believes are user-friendly and visually appealing. However, client feedback has just landed in her inbox, and it's filled with comments, suggestions, and sometimes, contradictions. Rachel knows that interpreting this feedback and making the right refinements is crucial to meeting project requirements and client expectations.

"ChatGPT, I need help making sense of this feedback," Rachel confides in the AI. ChatGPT responds with its characteristic assurance, "Of course, Rachel. Let's start by breaking down the feedback into categories: usability, aesthetics, and functionality. Then, we can prioritize the issues and address them systematically."

With ChatGPT's initial guidance, Rachel begins to dissect the feedback. She identifies common themes and recurring concerns. The AI recommends creating a feedback matrix, categorizing comments by priority and impact. This visual aid helps her gain a clearer perspective on what needs attention first.

Now, Rachel faces the challenge of turning this feedback into actionable adjustments. ChatGPT suggests using AI-powered design tools to implement changes efficiently. Rachel can experiment with different design elements, layouts, and color schemes in real time, allowing her to visualize the impact of each adjustment.

As Rachel engages in an ongoing dialogue with ChatGPT, she refines her design iteratively. The AI provides suggestions based on design best practices, ensuring that her adjustments align with industry standards and client expectations. It even helps her create alternative versions of the app screens for A/B testing, optimizing the user experience further.

Through this collaborative process, Rachel gains insights that transcend mere design changes. She learns to decipher the underlying motivations behind the feedback and how it ties to the project's objectives. ChatGPT helps her navigate the delicate balance between creative expression and client requirements.

In the end, Rachel presents her refined app screens to the client. The adjustments made based on feedback not only meet project requirements but also exceed client expectations. The app is now more user-friendly, visually engaging, and aligned with the client's vision.

In conclusion, AI, personified by ChatGPT, transforms feedback interpretation and refinement into a collaborative journey. It helps designers like Rachel navigate the intricacies of client feedback by breaking it down, prioritizing adjustments, and providing real-time design support. As Rachel's experience illustrates, AI isn't just a tool; it's a partner in the creative process, ensuring that your designs evolve to meet project requirements and client expectations. Embrace AI's feedback interpretation and refinement capabilities, and watch your projects flourish with precision and excellence.

Task: Feedback Analysis

Analyzing feedback from clients or team members to identify areas for improvement

Example Prompt 1:
Can you provide specific examples of feedback you've received from clients or team members regarding our recent project? How did you address or implement this feedback, and what were the results?

Example Prompt 2:
What patterns or recurring themes have you noticed in the feedback you've received? How do you plan to address these areas for improvement in future projects?

Example Prompt 3:
Describe a time when you received constructive criticism from a client or team member. How did you use this feedback to make

positive changes or improvements in your work?

Example Prompt 4:
In what ways do you actively seek out feedback from clients or team members? How do you ensure that you are effectively analyzing and incorporating this feedback into your work processes?

Task: Design Refinement
Making adjustments to design elements based on feedback

Example Prompt 1:
Can you provide feedback on the color scheme and overall visual appeal of the design? I can make adjustments to ensure it aligns with your vision.

Example Prompt 2:
What specific elements of the design do you feel could be improved or refined? I'm here to make the necessary adjustments to enhance the overall aesthetic.

Example Prompt 3:
Do you have any suggestions for refining the typography and layout of the design? I'm open to making changes to ensure it meets your expectations.

Example Prompt 4:
I'd love to hear your thoughts on the overall composition and balance of the design. Any feedback you provide will help me refine and perfect the visual elements.

Task: Iterative Design Process
Implementing a cyclical process of receiving feedback, making changes, and seeking further feedback

Example Prompt 1:
How can I improve the visual hierarchy of this design to better

guide the viewer's attention? Any suggestions for rearranging elements or adjusting font sizes?

Example Prompt 2:
I've made some changes based on previous feedback, but I'm still unsure about the color scheme. Any thoughts on how I can make it more cohesive and visually appealing?

Example Prompt 3:
I've received feedback on the overall layout of the design, but I'm struggling to find the right balance between simplicity and complexity. Any ideas for refining the composition and adding or removing elements?

Example Prompt 4:
I've incorporated feedback on the user interface, but I'm looking for suggestions on how to enhance the user experience through interactive elements. Any ideas for incorporating animations or micro-interactions to improve usability?

Task: Client Communication

Communicating with clients to understand their feedback and make necessary adjustments

Example Prompt 1:
How would you describe the overall look and feel you envision for your project? Are there any specific colors, fonts, or design elements that you have in mind?

Example Prompt 2:
Can you provide examples of designs or styles that you admire or would like to incorporate into your project? This will help me better understand your preferences and vision.

Example Prompt 3:
What aspects of the current design do you feel are working well, and are there any areas that you would like to see adjusted or improved?

Example Prompt 4:
In what ways do you hope the design will resonate with your target audience or convey your brand message? Understanding your goals and objectives will help me tailor the design to meet your needs.

Task: Design Presentation

Creating visual presentations of design options for client review and feedback

Example Prompt 1:
Create a visual presentation showcasing three different design options for a new logo, incorporating the client's brand colors and aesthetic preferences.

Example Prompt 2:
Design a series of visual mockups for a website homepage, highlighting various layout and color scheme options for the client to review and provide feedback on.

Example Prompt 3:
Develop a visual presentation of packaging design concepts for a new product, including different color schemes, typography, and imagery to present to the client for feedback.

Example Prompt 4:
Produce a visual presentation of interior design options for a client's office space, incorporating different furniture layouts, color palettes, and decorative elements for review and feedback.

Task: Design Testing

Conducting user testing and gathering feedback on design prototypes

Example Prompt 1:
How can we improve the user experience of this design prototype? Please provide specific feedback on the layout, color scheme, and

overall usability.

Example Prompt 2:
What elements of this design prototype do you find most appealing and why? Are there any aspects that you find confusing or difficult to navigate?

Example Prompt 3:
Please share your thoughts on the visual hierarchy of this design prototype. Do you feel that the most important elements are emphasized effectively? If not, how could we improve this?

Example Prompt 4:
As you interact with this design prototype, please take note of any areas where you encounter usability issues or confusion. Your feedback will help us refine and optimize the user experience.

Task: Design Evaluation

Evaluating the effectiveness of design solutions based on feedback and making refinements as needed

Example Prompt 1:
Can you provide feedback on the overall visual impact of this design? Are there any elements that stand out to you as particularly effective or ineffective?

Example Prompt 2:
How does the design solution align with the intended message or brand identity? Are there any areas where the design could be strengthened to better convey the desired message?

Example Prompt 3:
In terms of user experience, how intuitive and easy to navigate is the design? Are there any areas where the user may encounter confusion or difficulty?

Example Prompt 4:
Based on the feedback received, what refinements or adjustments

do you believe would enhance the overall effectiveness of the design solution?

Task: Design Documentation

Documenting feedback and changes made to designs for future reference and improvement.

Example Prompt 1:
Create a chatGPT prompt that guides the user to document the feedback received on a specific design project, including the source of the feedback, the nature of the feedback, and any suggested changes or improvements.

Example Prompt 2:
Develop a prompt that encourages the user to outline the specific changes made to a design based on feedback received, including before and after comparisons, rationale for the changes, and the impact on the overall design.

Example Prompt 3:
Craft a chatGPT prompt that prompts the user to create a comprehensive design documentation template, including sections for recording feedback, proposed changes, implemented changes, and the overall impact on the design's effectiveness.

Example Prompt 4:
Design a prompt that guides the user to document the iterative design process, including initial design concepts, feedback received at each stage, changes made in response to feedback, and the final outcome of the design project.

Idea: Feedback Survey Design

Create visually appealing feedback surveys for clients to gather input on design projects.

Example Prompt 1:
Prompt: "ChatGPT, as a graphic designer, I need your support to

create visually appealing feedback surveys for clients to gather input on design projects. Can you help me design a survey template that reflects our brand's aesthetic and is easy for clients to navigate?"

Example Prompt 2:

Prompt: "As a graphic designer, I'm looking to enhance our feedback survey design process. ChatGPT, can you assist me in developing interactive and engaging survey layouts that capture the attention of our clients and encourage them to provide detailed feedback on our design projects?"

Example Prompt 3:

Prompt: "ChatGPT, I need your expertise as a graphic designer to help me craft feedback surveys that not only look visually appealing but also effectively communicate the purpose of gathering input on design projects. Can you assist me in creating survey questions and response options that are clear and easy to understand?"

Example Prompt 4:

Prompt: "As a graphic designer, I want to elevate our feedback survey design to better showcase our creativity and attention to detail. ChatGPT, can you collaborate with me to develop innovative and visually stunning survey graphics that align with our brand's design principles and leave a lasting impression on our clients?"

Idea: Feedback Analysis Infographics

Use ChatGPT to help interpret and visualize feedback data in the form of infographics for easy understanding.

Example Prompt 1:

Create an infographic that visually represents the sentiment analysis of customer feedback for our latest product launch. Use ChatGPT to analyze the feedback data and present it in a visually appealing and easy-to-understand format.

Example Prompt 2:

Design an infographic that showcases the key themes and trends identified in the feedback from our recent customer survey. Utilize ChatGPT to analyze the survey responses and translate the data into a visually engaging infographic.

Example Prompt 3:

Develop an infographic that illustrates the comparative analysis of feedback from different customer segments. Leverage ChatGPT to analyze the feedback data and present the insights in a visually compelling and informative infographic.

Example Prompt 4:

Produce an infographic that highlights the most common issues and positive feedback themes identified in customer reviews. Utilize ChatGPT to analyze the review data and create an infographic that effectively communicates the key insights.

Idea: Client Feedback Presentation Templates

Design customizable presentation templates for sharing feedback interpretations with clients.

Example Prompt 1:

Create a set of customizable presentation templates specifically tailored for sharing client feedback interpretations. The templates should include visually appealing layouts and graphics to effectively communicate the feedback analysis to clients.

Example Prompt 2:

Design a series of client feedback presentation templates that can be easily personalized with company branding and client-specific data. The templates should be versatile enough to accommodate various types of feedback, from survey results to performance evaluations.

Example Prompt 3:

Develop a range of visually engaging presentation templates for presenting client feedback in a clear and professional manner. The templates should incorporate infographics, charts, and other visual elements to effectively convey the key insights and recommendations derived from the feedback.

Example Prompt 4:
Produce a collection of customizable presentation templates that are specifically designed for sharing client feedback interpretations. The templates should be easy to edit and should include placeholders for client logos, project details, and key findings to streamline the process of presenting feedback to clients.

Idea: Feedback Interpretation Consultation

Offer services to interpret and refine client feedback to improve design projects.

Example Prompt 1:
ChatGPT, I need your assistance in interpreting and refining client feedback for my design projects. Can you help me analyze and understand the feedback to make necessary improvements?

Example Prompt 2:
As a graphic designer, I often struggle with interpreting client feedback to enhance my design projects. Can you provide guidance on how to effectively interpret and refine feedback to achieve better results?

Example Prompt 3:
I'm looking for support in understanding and refining client feedback for my design work. Can you assist me in analyzing the feedback and suggesting ways to improve my designs based on the input received?

Example Prompt 4:
I need help in interpreting and refining client feedback to enhance my design projects. Can you provide consultation on how to effectively interpret feedback and make necessary adjustments to

improve the overall design?

Idea: Feedback Dashboard Design

Create interactive dashboards to track and visualize feedback data for ongoing design projects.

Example Prompt 1:
Design a user-friendly feedback dashboard interface that allows for easy visualization of feedback data from various design projects. The dashboard should include interactive elements such as filters, charts, and graphs to help track and analyze feedback trends.

Example Prompt 2:
Develop a customizable feedback dashboard template that can be easily integrated into different design projects. The template should allow for the input of feedback data and provide options for visualizing the data in a clear and concise manner.

Example Prompt 3:
Create a feedback dashboard with the ability to track and compare feedback data over time, allowing for the identification of patterns and trends in user feedback. The dashboard should also include features for exporting and sharing feedback reports with project stakeholders.

Example Prompt 4:
Design an intuitive feedback dashboard that can be accessed and updated in real-time, providing designers with immediate insights into user feedback. The dashboard should be visually appealing and easy to navigate, with options for customizing the display of feedback data based on project requirements.

Idea: Feedback Interpretation Workshops

Host workshops to teach clients how to interpret and refine feedback for better design outcomes.

Example Prompt 1:
Create a workshop outline and presentation slides for a Feedback Interpretation Workshop, focusing on teaching clients how to interpret and refine feedback for better design outcomes. Include interactive activities and examples to engage participants.

Example Prompt 2:
Design a series of promotional materials for the Feedback Interpretation Workshops, including social media graphics, flyers, and email templates. The materials should effectively communicate the benefits of attending the workshops and encourage participation.

Example Prompt 3:
Develop a comprehensive curriculum for the Feedback Interpretation Workshops, outlining the key topics to be covered, learning objectives, and suggested activities. The curriculum should be structured to provide a clear and engaging learning experience for participants.

Example Prompt 4:
Produce a set of visual aids and resources for the Feedback Interpretation Workshops, such as infographics, handouts, and presentation templates. These resources should help to reinforce key concepts and provide valuable reference materials for workshop participants.

Idea: Feedback Interpretation Case Studies

Use ChatGPT to help create case studies showcasing successful feedback interpretation and refinement.

Example Prompt 1:
Create a case study highlighting how ChatGPT was used to interpret and refine customer feedback for a popular product or service. Include examples of how the AI helped identify key themes and sentiments within the feedback data.

Example Prompt 2:
Utilize ChatGPT to analyze and present a case study on how feedback interpretation led to significant improvements in a company's customer satisfaction ratings. Showcase specific examples of how the AI assisted in understanding and addressing customer concerns.

Example Prompt 3:
Develop a case study demonstrating how ChatGPT was employed to interpret and refine feedback from a beta testing group, leading to successful product enhancements and feature adjustments. Highlight the specific insights and recommendations provided by the AI.

Example Prompt 4:
Use ChatGPT to create a case study illustrating how feedback interpretation played a crucial role in the development and refinement of a new software application. Showcase how the AI helped identify and prioritize user feedback, leading to a more user-friendly and effective product.

Idea: Feedback Interpretation Webinars

Host webinars to educate other designers on the importance of feedback interpretation and refinement.

Example Prompt 1:
Create a promotional graphic for an upcoming webinar on feedback interpretation for designers. The graphic should include the webinar title, date, time, and a visually appealing design that conveys the importance of feedback interpretation in the design process.

Example Prompt 2:
Design a series of social media graphics to promote the feedback interpretation webinars. These graphics should be eye-catching and informative, highlighting the key benefits of attending the

webinar and encouraging other designers to join.

Example Prompt 3:

Develop a visually engaging presentation template for the feedback interpretation webinars. The template should include placeholders for text, images, and data visualization, as well as a cohesive design that reflects the importance of feedback interpretation in the design industry.

Example Prompt 4:

Design an interactive landing page for the feedback interpretation webinars. The landing page should feature compelling visuals, clear calls-to-action, and an intuitive layout that encourages designers to sign up for the webinar and learn more about the importance of feedback interpretation in their work.

Idea: Feedback Interpretation Tools

Develop tools or resources to assist designers in interpreting and refining feedback from clients.

Example Prompt 1:

Create a tool or resource that helps designers interpret and refine feedback from clients, allowing them to better understand and implement client suggestions and preferences in their designs.

Example Prompt 2:

Design a system that can analyze and categorize client feedback, providing designers with actionable insights and suggestions for refining their work based on client input.

Example Prompt 3:

Develop a visual feedback interpretation tool that can help designers translate client comments and critiques into specific design adjustments, streamlining the feedback process and improving client satisfaction.

Example Prompt 4:

Produce a set of templates or guidelines for designers to use when interpreting and responding to client feedback, offering best practices and strategies for effectively incorporating client input into their design work.

Idea: Feedback Interpretation Blog Series

Create a series of blog posts discussing different aspects of feedback interpretation and refinement in graphic design.

Example Prompt 1:

Can you help me outline a series of blog posts on feedback interpretation in graphic design? I'd like to cover topics such as understanding client feedback, incorporating constructive criticism, and refining design based on feedback. Let's brainstorm some key points for each post.

Example Prompt 2:

I'm looking to create a blog series focused on feedback interpretation in graphic design. Can you assist me in designing visually appealing graphics and illustrations to accompany each post? I want the visuals to effectively convey the concepts discussed in the text.

Example Prompt 3:

I need support in researching and compiling examples of successful feedback interpretation in graphic design for my blog series. Can you help me gather case studies and real-life examples that demonstrate the impact of refining designs based on feedback?

Example Prompt 4:

I'm seeking assistance in creating a cohesive visual identity for my blog series on feedback interpretation in graphic design. Can you help me design a logo, color scheme, and overall aesthetic that reflects the theme of the series and appeals to my target audience?

Idea: Feedback Interpretation Podcast

Start a podcast discussing real-world examples and tips for

interpreting and refining feedback in graphic design.

Example Prompt 1:

Create a script for the first episode of a podcast series focused on interpreting and refining feedback in graphic design. Include real-world examples and tips for graphic designers to improve their work based on feedback.

Example Prompt 2:

Design a logo and cover art for a podcast series titled 'Feedback Interpretation in Graphic Design'. The design should be visually appealing and convey the theme of interpreting and refining feedback in the graphic design industry.

Example Prompt 3:

Develop a promotional graphic for the launch of a new podcast series about feedback interpretation in graphic design. The graphic should include key details such as the podcast title, release date, and a brief description of what listeners can expect.

Example Prompt 4:

Brainstorm and outline potential guest speakers or industry experts to feature on the podcast series about interpreting and refining feedback in graphic design. Consider individuals with experience in giving and receiving feedback in the design field.

Idea: Feedback Interpretation Software Integration

Work on integrating ChatGPT into design software to assist with interpreting and refining feedback in real-time.

Example Prompt 1:

ChatGPT, can you help design software by integrating a feature that allows for real-time interpretation and refinement of feedback from users? This would greatly improve the efficiency and accuracy of the design process.

Example Prompt 2:

I need ChatGPT to assist in the development of a feedback interpretation software integration for design tools. Can you provide support in creating a system that can analyze and interpret feedback from users to help refine and improve designs in real-time?

Example Prompt 3:

As a graphic designer, I'm looking to integrate ChatGPT into design software to assist with interpreting and refining feedback in real-time. Can you help in developing a solution that seamlessly integrates natural language processing to enhance the design process?

Example Prompt 4:

ChatGPT, I need your expertise in integrating real-time feedback interpretation software into design tools. Can you assist in creating a system that can analyze and interpret user feedback to provide valuable insights for refining and improving designs on the fly?

DIGITAL ASSET MANAGEMENT

ORGANIZED CREATIVITY: DIGITAL ASSET MANAGEMENT

In the fast-paced world of graphic design, digital asset management is the bedrock of efficiency and consistency. This chapter unveils the transformative potential of AI, embodied by ChatGPT, in the realm of digital asset management. Join us as we follow the journey of Michael, a seasoned graphic designer, in his quest to streamline his workflow and maintain design consistency.

Michael is knee-deep in a project that involves designing marketing materials for a global client with diverse branding assets. He knows that managing fonts, templates, and images efficiently is key to delivering top-notch work. ChatGPT emerges as his trusted ally, ready to provide invaluable insights.

"ChatGPT, I need a strategy for organizing and managing these digital assets effectively," Michael shares his challenge. ChatGPT responds with a confident tone, "Certainly, Michael. Let's start by categorizing assets based on their type and purpose. Then, we can establish a clear naming convention and leverage AI-powered tagging for easy search and retrieval."

With ChatGPT's initial guidance, Michael begins the process of organizing his digital assets. He creates folders for fonts, templates, and images, and subfolders for each project to maintain clarity. The AI suggests a standardized naming convention that includes project name, date, and asset type, ensuring consistency across the board.

Now, Michael faces the daunting task of tagging each asset for quick access. ChatGPT recommends using AI-powered tagging tools that can automatically recognize and assign relevant keywords to images and templates. This saves him countless hours of manual tagging and ensures that assets are easily retrievable.

As Michael continues the conversation with ChatGPT, he explores version control techniques to manage ongoing design iterations efficiently. The AI suggests using cloud-based solutions that enable real-time collaboration and version history tracking. This ensures that everyone on the team is working with the latest assets.

But digital asset management isn't just about organization; it's about accessibility. ChatGPT recommends creating a centralized digital asset library accessible to all team members, ensuring that everyone is on the same page and can access the necessary resources effortlessly.

Through this collaborative process, Michael transforms his digital asset management approach. He can now locate fonts, templates, and images in seconds, regardless of project size or complexity. His workflow becomes streamlined, allowing him to focus more on creative aspects and less on asset hunting.

In conclusion, AI, embodied by ChatGPT, revolutionizes digital asset management for graphic designers like Michael. It offers actionable strategies for organizing and managing digital assets efficiently, ensuring that workflows are streamlined, and design consistency is maintained. As Michael's experience illustrates, AI isn't just a tool; it's a partner in the creative process, enhancing productivity and elevating the quality of work. Embrace AI in your digital asset management, and watch your efficiency and consistency soar to new heights.

Task: File organization

Help in creating a system for organizing digital files and assets

Example Prompt 1:
Can you suggest a visually appealing folder structure for organizing design files, such as separating by project, client, and file type?

Example Prompt 2:
How can I effectively label and tag my design assets to make them easily searchable and accessible within a digital asset management system?

Example Prompt 3:
What are some best practices for version control and naming conventions to keep track of iterations and updates for design files?

Example Prompt 4:
I'm looking for ideas on how to visually categorize and group design assets within a cloud-based storage system for easy navigation and retrieval. Any suggestions?

Task: Metadata tagging

Assist in adding relevant metadata to digital assets for easy search and retrieval

Example Prompt 1:
How can we ensure that our digital assets are properly tagged with relevant metadata to improve searchability and retrieval?

Example Prompt 2:
What are some best practices for adding metadata to our digital assets to make them more easily searchable?

Example Prompt 3:
Can you provide some examples of effective metadata tagging strategies for different types of digital assets, such as images, videos, and documents?

Example Prompt 4:
What tools or software do you recommend for efficiently adding and managing metadata for our digital assets?

Task: Version control

Provide support in managing different versions of digital assets

Example Prompt 1:
How can I effectively manage different versions of my design files to ensure smooth collaboration and avoid confusion among team members?

Example Prompt 2:
What are some best practices for implementing version control for graphic design projects, especially when working with multiple stakeholders or clients?

Example Prompt 3:
Can you recommend any specific tools or software that are particularly useful for version control and managing different iterations of design files?

Example Prompt 4:
What strategies can I use to track changes and updates to my design files, and how can I ensure that the most current version is always easily accessible to the team?

Task: Access control

Help in setting permissions and access levels for different users

Example Prompt 1:
How can I create different user roles with specific access levels in my system? I need to ensure that certain users have limited access to sensitive information.

Example Prompt 2:
I'm looking for guidance on setting up access control for a new project. What are the best practices for managing permissions and access levels for different user groups?

Example Prompt 3:
I need assistance in implementing access control measures to restrict certain users from modifying critical data. What are the recommended strategies for achieving this?

Example Prompt 4:
Can you provide examples of how to use access control lists (ACLs) to manage user permissions and access levels within a network environment?

Task: File conversion

Assist in converting digital files to different formats as needed

Example Prompt 1:
Can you help me convert a PDF file to a Word document? I need to make some edits to the text.

Example Prompt 2:

I have a JPEG image that I need to convert to a PNG with a transparent background. Can you assist with that?

Example Prompt 3:
I'm trying to convert a video file from MOV to MP4. Can you recommend a reliable file conversion tool or software?

Example Prompt 4:
I need to convert a large batch of images from TIFF to JPEG. What's the most efficient way to do this without losing quality?

Task: Search and retrieval

Provide tools for easy searching and retrieval of digital assets

Example Prompt 1:
Create a user-friendly interface for searching and retrieving digital assets, incorporating advanced filters and sorting options to streamline the process.

Example Prompt 2:
Design a visually appealing and intuitive search bar that allows users to easily input keywords and find relevant digital assets quickly.

Example Prompt 3:
Develop a system for tagging and categorizing digital assets to improve search accuracy and efficiency, ensuring that users can easily locate the exact files they need.

Example Prompt 4:
Incorporate thumbnail previews and detailed metadata display options to assist users in visually identifying and selecting the right digital assets during the retrieval process.

Task: Backup and recovery

Assist in setting up backup systems and recovering lost digital assets

Example Prompt 1:
Can you provide step-by-step instructions for setting up an automated backup system for my digital files and assets?

Example Prompt 2:
What are the best practices for ensuring the security and reliability of my backup system for digital assets?

Example Prompt 3:
How can I recover lost digital assets from a backup system in the event of a data loss or system failure?

Example Prompt 4:
Can you recommend any software or tools that can help streamline the backup and recovery process for digital assets?

Task: Usage tracking

Help in tracking the usage and performance of digital assets

Example Prompt 1:
How can I design a visually appealing usage tracking dashboard to monitor the performance of our digital assets?

Example Prompt 2:
What are some effective graphic design techniques for creating usage tracking visualizations and infographics?

Example Prompt 3:
Can you provide examples of how to incorporate usage tracking data into our digital asset designs to improve user engagement?

Example Prompt 4:
What are the best practices for visually representing usage tracking data in a way that is easy for stakeholders to understand and interpret?

Task: Collaboration tools

Provide tools for collaborative work on digital assets

Example Prompt 1:

What are some effective collaboration tools for graphic designers to work on digital assets together in real-time?

Example Prompt 2:

Can you recommend any platforms or software that allow for seamless collaboration on design projects, such as sharing and editing digital assets simultaneously?

Example Prompt 3:

How do graphic designers effectively use collaborative tools to streamline the process of creating and editing digital assets with team members or clients?

Example Prompt 4:

What are some best practices for utilizing collaborative tools in graphic design projects to ensure efficient communication and seamless workflow when working on digital assets?

Task: Integration with design software

Assist in integrating digital asset management with design software for seamless workflow.

Example Prompt 1:

How can design software be optimized to seamlessly integrate with digital asset management systems for efficient file organization and access?

Example Prompt 2:

What are the best practices for integrating design software with digital asset management to ensure a smooth workflow for graphic designers?

Example Prompt 3:

Can you provide tips and tricks for streamlining the integration of design software with digital asset management to improve collaboration and productivity?

Example Prompt 4:
What are the potential challenges and solutions for integrating design software with digital asset management systems to enhance the overall design process?

Idea: Brand asset organization

Use ChatGPT to create a system for organizing and categorizing brand assets such as logos, color palettes, and fonts for easy access and retrieval.

Example Prompt 1:
Prompt: "As a Graphic Designer, I need help organizing and categorizing brand assets such as logos, color palettes, and fonts for easy access and retrieval. Can you help me create a system for this using ChatGPT?"

Example Prompt 2:
Prompt: "I'm looking to streamline the organization of brand assets like logos, color palettes, and fonts. Can ChatGPT assist me in creating a system that allows for easy access and retrieval of these assets?"

Example Prompt 3:
Prompt: "As a Graphic Designer, I'm seeking a solution to efficiently organize and categorize brand assets such as logos, color palettes, and fonts. Can ChatGPT help me develop a system for this purpose?"

Example Prompt 4:
Prompt: "I'm in need of a system to effectively manage and categorize brand assets like logos, color palettes, and fonts. Can ChatGPT support me in creating a solution for easy access and retrieval of these assets?"

Idea: Digital asset tagging

Utilize ChatGPT to develop a tagging system for digital assets to improve searchability and categorization.

Example Prompt 1:
Create a system for tagging digital assets based on content and context, allowing for easier search and categorization within a digital library or database.

Example Prompt 2:
Design a user-friendly interface for adding and managing tags for various types of digital assets, such as images, videos, and documents.

Example Prompt 3:
Develop a machine learning algorithm that can suggest relevant tags for digital assets based on their content and metadata, improving the efficiency of the tagging process.

Example Prompt 4:
Integrate the tagging system with existing digital asset management platforms to streamline the organization and retrieval of digital assets across different departments or teams.

Idea: Asset version control

Implement a version control system for digital assets using ChatGPT to track changes and updates.

Example Prompt 1:
Design a user-friendly interface for a digital asset version control system, ensuring easy navigation and clear visibility of version history and updates.

Example Prompt 2:
Create a visual representation of the version control process, illustrating how ChatGPT can track changes and updates for digital assets.

Example Prompt 3:

Design a set of icons and graphics to represent different versions of digital assets within the version control system, making it easy for users to identify and manage their assets.

Example Prompt 4:
Develop a series of infographics explaining the benefits and features of using ChatGPT for digital asset version control, highlighting its efficiency and accuracy in tracking changes and updates.

Idea: Asset metadata creation

Use ChatGPT to generate metadata for digital assets, including descriptions, keywords, and usage rights.

Example Prompt 1:
Prompt: "Hey ChatGPT, as a graphic designer, I need help creating metadata for my digital assets. Can you assist me in generating detailed descriptions, relevant keywords, and usage rights for my images, illustrations, and designs?"

Example Prompt 2:
Prompt: "ChatGPT, I'm looking for support in creating metadata for my digital assets. Can you help me generate accurate and comprehensive descriptions, relevant keywords, and usage rights information for my graphic design work?"

Example Prompt 3:
Prompt: "As a graphic designer, I need assistance in generating metadata for my digital assets. Can you help me create detailed descriptions, relevant keywords, and usage rights information for my images, illustrations, and designs using your language generation capabilities?"

Example Prompt 4:
Prompt: "Hey ChatGPT, I'm seeking your help as a graphic designer to generate metadata for my digital assets. Can you support me in creating comprehensive descriptions, relevant keywords, and usage

rights information for my graphic design work?"

Idea: Asset approval workflow

Develop a workflow for approving and reviewing digital assets using ChatGPT to streamline the process.

Example Prompt 1:
Design a user-friendly interface for a digital asset approval workflow, incorporating ChatGPT to facilitate communication and decision-making among team members.

Example Prompt 2:
Create a visual representation of the digital asset approval process, integrating ChatGPT as a virtual assistant to guide users through each step.

Example Prompt 3:
Develop a set of customizable templates for digital asset approval forms, with ChatGPT providing real-time feedback and suggestions for improvement.

Example Prompt 4:
Design a series of informative graphics and illustrations to accompany the digital asset approval workflow, with ChatGPT providing explanations and tips for efficient use.

Idea: Asset usage tracking

Utilize ChatGPT to create a system for tracking the usage and performance of digital assets across different platforms.

Example Prompt 1:
Create a system for tracking the usage and performance of digital assets across different platforms, including social media, websites, and advertising campaigns. Provide a detailed breakdown of how ChatGPT can assist in analyzing and reporting on the effectiveness of each asset.

Example Prompt 2:
Develop a method for monitoring the engagement and reach of digital assets such as images, videos, and infographics across various online channels. Explain how ChatGPT can be utilized to automate the process of collecting and analyzing data to provide insights into asset performance.

Example Prompt 3:
Design a solution for tracking the usage and impact of digital assets in real-time, allowing for immediate adjustments and optimizations. Describe how ChatGPT can be integrated into this system to provide ongoing monitoring and reporting on asset performance.

Example Prompt 4:
Devise a strategy for identifying trends and patterns in the usage of digital assets, enabling proactive decision-making and strategic planning. Explain how ChatGPT can be leveraged to analyze data and provide actionable insights for improving the performance of assets across different platforms.

Idea: Asset rights management

Implement a system for managing usage rights and permissions for digital assets using ChatGPT to automate the process.

Example Prompt 1:
Design a user-friendly interface for a digital asset rights management system, incorporating features for tracking usage rights and permissions. Use ChatGPT to generate sample user feedback and suggestions for improvement.

Example Prompt 2:
Create a visual identity and branding elements for a digital asset rights management platform, ensuring that the design reflects the concept of secure and efficient usage rights management. Use

ChatGPT to brainstorm creative ideas for the branding and visual elements.

Example Prompt 3:
Develop a series of infographics and visual guides to explain the process of digital asset rights management, using ChatGPT to generate clear and concise explanations of complex concepts.

Example Prompt 4:
Design a set of customizable templates for digital asset usage rights agreements, incorporating ChatGPT-generated language that clearly outlines permissions and restrictions for various types of digital assets.

Idea: Asset collaboration platform

Use ChatGPT to develop a platform for collaborating on digital asset creation and management with team members and clients.

Example Prompt 1:
Prompt: "ChatGPT, can you help design a user-friendly interface for an asset collaboration platform that allows team members and clients to upload, share, and collaborate on digital assets such as images, videos, and design files?"

Example Prompt 2:
Prompt: "ChatGPT, please assist in creating a feature that allows users to leave comments and feedback directly on digital assets within the collaboration platform, facilitating seamless communication and collaboration."

Example Prompt 3:
Prompt: "ChatGPT, can you help develop a system for version control and asset management within the collaboration platform, allowing users to track changes, revert to previous versions, and maintain organized digital asset libraries?"

Example Prompt 4:

Prompt: "ChatGPT, please assist in designing a secure and customizable permission system for the asset collaboration platform, allowing users to control access levels and permissions for team members and clients to ensure data security and privacy."

Idea: Asset archiving and retrieval

Create a system for archiving and retrieving digital assets using ChatGPT to ensure easy access and organization.

Example Prompt 1:
Design a user-friendly interface for a digital asset archiving and retrieval system, ensuring easy navigation and efficient organization of files.

Example Prompt 2:
Develop a system for tagging and categorizing digital assets based on content and metadata, allowing for quick and accurate retrieval using ChatGPT's natural language processing capabilities.

Example Prompt 3:
Create a visually appealing and intuitive search function that utilizes ChatGPT to understand and interpret user queries, providing relevant results for digital asset retrieval.

Example Prompt 4:
Design a customizable dashboard for users to manage and access their archived digital assets, integrating ChatGPT for personalized recommendations and smart organization features.

Idea: Asset format conversion

Utilize ChatGPT to automate the conversion of digital assets to different formats for various platforms and devices.

Example Prompt 1:
ChatGPT, can you help me create a script to automate the conversion of images and videos to different formats such as JPEG,

PNG, MP4, and GIF for optimal display on various platforms and devices?

Example Prompt 2:
I need assistance in developing a system using ChatGPT to convert vector graphics to SVG, EPS, and PDF formats for seamless integration across different design software and web platforms. Can you help with this?

Example Prompt 3:
ChatGPT, I'm looking to streamline the process of converting audio files to MP3, WAV, and AIFF formats for compatibility with different devices and streaming platforms. Can you assist in creating a conversion automation script?

Example Prompt 4:
As a graphic designer, I often need to convert large batches of files to different formats for client deliverables. Can ChatGPT help me develop a solution to automate the conversion of images, videos, and audio files to meet various platform requirements?

Idea: Asset backup and recovery

Implement a backup and recovery system for digital assets using ChatGPT to ensure data security and continuity.

Example Prompt 1:
Prompt: "Design a user-friendly interface for a digital asset backup and recovery system. Provide step-by-step instructions for users to easily navigate and utilize the system. Include visual elements such as icons and graphics to enhance the user experience."

Example Prompt 2:
Prompt: "Create a series of infographics explaining the importance of digital asset backup and recovery, highlighting potential risks and consequences of data loss. Use engaging visuals and concise messaging to effectively communicate the need for a reliable backup system."

Example Prompt 3:
Prompt: *"Develop a set of customizable templates for digital asset backup plans, tailored to different types of businesses and industries. Incorporate visually appealing elements and clear, easy-to-follow instructions for users to create their own backup and recovery strategies."*

Example Prompt 4:
Prompt: *"Design a promotional campaign to raise awareness about the benefits of using ChatGPT for digital asset backup and recovery. Create visually striking social media graphics, banners, and advertisements to showcase the reliability and security of the system, encouraging businesses and individuals to safeguard their valuable data."*

Idea: Asset performance analysis

Use ChatGPT to analyze the performance of digital assets and provide insights for optimization and improvement.

Example Prompt 1:

Prompt: *"Hey ChatGPT, as a graphic designer, I need your help to analyze the performance of my digital assets. Can you provide insights on how to optimize and improve the engagement and effectiveness of my designs?"*

Example Prompt 2:
Prompt: *"ChatGPT, I'm looking to enhance the performance of my digital assets as a graphic designer. Can you analyze the current engagement levels and provide suggestions for improvement and optimization?"*

Example Prompt 3:
Prompt: *"As a graphic designer, I'm seeking your support, ChatGPT, to analyze the performance of my digital assets. Can you provide insights and recommendations for optimizing and improving the effectiveness of my designs?"*

Example Prompt 4:

Prompt: "ChatGPT, I need your assistance as a graphic designer to analyze the performance of my digital assets. Can you help me identify areas for improvement and provide insights on how to optimize the engagement and impact of my designs?"

SOCIAL MEDIA GRAPHICS

VIRAL VISUALS: DESIGNING FOR SOCIAL MEDIA

In the dynamic landscape of graphic design, crafting social media graphics that resonate with audiences is both an art and a science. This chapter unveils how AI, embodied by ChatGPT, can be your strategic ally in creating optimized graphics for various social media platforms. Follow the journey of Jessica, a talented graphic designer, as she navigates the intricacies of social media graphic design with ChatGPT by her side.

Jessica is tasked with creating eye-catching graphics for a client's social media campaign. Each platform, be it Facebook, Instagram, Twitter, or LinkedIn, comes with its own set of dimension requirements, resolutions, and best practices. Jessica knows that tailoring her designs to these specifications is crucial for engagement and success.

"ChatGPT, I need to create graphics that perform well on different social media platforms. Can you help?" Jessica turns to the AI for guidance. ChatGPT responds confidently, "Of course, Jessica. Let's start by breaking down the key platforms and their optimal graphic dimensions. From there, we can explore design strategies to make your visuals stand out."

With ChatGPT's initial guidance, Jessica begins her journey into the world of social media graphics. She compiles a list of platform-specific dimension requirements, ensuring she has the correct canvas sizes for each. The AI suggests creating templates with these dimensions, making it easier to maintain consistency across the campaign.

Now, Jessica faces the challenge of adapting her designs to each platform's unique audience and content style. ChatGPT recommends researching each platform's best practices, such as using hashtags on Instagram or concise messaging on Twitter. This ensures that her graphics align with the platform's culture and maximize engagement.

But it's not just about dimensions and content. ChatGPT encourages Jessica to experiment with AI-driven design tools that can automatically adjust graphics to fit different platforms. This saves her valuable time and effort while maintaining the integrity of her designs.

As Jessica continues the conversation with ChatGPT, she explores the importance of visual storytelling in social media graphics. The AI suggests using captivating imagery, concise text, and a strong call to action to drive engagement. Jessica learns how to leverage AI for image enhancement, ensuring that her visuals are attention-grabbing and shareable.

Through this collaborative process, Jessica transforms her approach to social media graphic design. She can now create optimized graphics for various platforms with ease, ensuring that her client's campaign thrives in the competitive landscape of social media.

In conclusion, AI, embodied by ChatGPT, becomes an indispensable partner for graphic designers like Jessica in the realm of social media graphics. It offers valuable insights into platform-specific dimensions, resolutions, and best practices while introducing AI-driven design tools for efficiency. As Jessica's journey illustrates, AI isn't just a tool; it's a strategist, enhancing the impact of your social media graphics and helping you connect with your audience effectively. Embrace AI in your social media graphic design, and watch your campaigns soar to new heights of engagement and success.

Note: Within this chapter, you may find it beneficial to employ AI for creating essential images that complement the strategies, tasks, and ideas. For more details, refer to my video training on: jeroenerne.com/AI-images

Task: Creating social media post templates

Designing customizable templates for various social media platforms

Example Prompt 1:

Design a social media post template that incorporates our brand colors and logo, with space for a compelling headline and engaging imagery.

Example Prompt 2:

Create a customizable template for Instagram stories that includes options for different photo layouts and text styles to highlight our latest promotions or products.

Example Prompt 3:

Develop a series of templates for Facebook posts that can be easily

customized with different background images and text styles to showcase customer testimonials or success stories.

Example Prompt 4:
Design a set of templates for Twitter posts that feature eye-catching graphics and space for short, impactful messages to drive engagement and conversation around our brand.

Task: Designing infographics for social media

Creating visually appealing and informative infographics for social media posts

Example Prompt 1:
Create an infographic that visually explains the benefits of using our product or service, using a color scheme that aligns with our brand identity.

Example Prompt 2:
Design an infographic that showcases key statistics or data points related to our industry, using engaging visuals and easy-to-read charts or graphs.

Example Prompt 3:
Develop an infographic that educates our audience on a complex topic or process, breaking it down into digestible, visually appealing sections.

Example Prompt 4:
Craft an infographic that highlights customer testimonials or success stories, incorporating compelling visuals and quotes to grab attention on social media.

Task: Designing cover photos and profile pictures

Crafting eye-catching cover photos and profile pictures for social media profiles

Example Prompt 1:
Create a cover photo that captures the essence of the brand or individual's personality, using vibrant colors and bold typography to make a statement on social media profiles.

Example Prompt 2:
Design a profile picture that incorporates the brand's logo or personal image in a visually appealing way, ensuring it stands out and is easily recognizable in a crowded social media feed.

Example Prompt 3:
Craft a cover photo that tells a story or conveys a message about the brand or individual, using imagery and composition to draw in viewers and create a lasting impression.

Example Prompt 4:
Develop a profile picture that exudes professionalism and approachability, using clean lines and modern design elements to create a polished and inviting visual presence on social media platforms.

Task: Designing quote graphics

Creating visually appealing graphics featuring quotes for social media posts

Example Prompt 1:
Design a visually striking graphic featuring the quote 'Creativity is intelligence having fun' by Albert Einstein, suitable for sharing on Instagram and Pinterest.

Example Prompt 2:
Create a quote graphic with the phrase 'The only way to do great work is to love what you do' by Steve Jobs, using a modern and minimalist design aesthetic for use on Twitter and Facebook.

Example Prompt 3:
Design a visually appealing graphic featuring the quote 'In every

job that must be done, there is an element of fun' from Mary Poppins, with a whimsical and playful style for sharing on Instagram Stories and Snapchat.

Example Prompt 4:
Create a quote graphic with the phrase 'The future belongs to those who believe in the beauty of their dreams' by Eleanor Roosevelt, using a bold and eye-catching typography for use on LinkedIn and Tumblr.

Task: Designing promotional graphics
Developing graphics for promotional purposes on social media

Example Prompt 1:
Create a series of eye-catching social media graphics to promote our upcoming product launch. Incorporate our brand colors and logo for a cohesive look.

Example Prompt 2:
Design a set of promotional graphics for our upcoming event, including banners, social media posts, and email headers. Emphasize the event's key details and use engaging visuals to capture attention.

Example Prompt 3:
Develop a series of graphics for our seasonal sale promotion, highlighting our best deals and special offers. Ensure the graphics are optimized for various social media platforms and can be easily shared by our audience.

Example Prompt 4:
Design a visually appealing infographic to showcase the benefits of our latest service offering. Use engaging visuals and concise text to effectively communicate the value proposition to our target audience.

Task: Designing event graphics

Creating graphics for promoting events on social media

Example Prompt 1:
Design a vibrant and eye-catching graphic for a music festival, incorporating elements of music, energy, and excitement to capture the attention of potential attendees on social media.

Example Prompt 2:
Create a series of graphics for a charity gala, using elegant and sophisticated design elements to convey the event's purpose and appeal to a high-end audience on social media.

Example Prompt 3:
Design a set of graphics for a business conference, utilizing professional and modern aesthetics to convey the event's focus on innovation and industry leadership for promotion on social media platforms.

Example Prompt 4:
Develop a visually engaging graphic for a community event, incorporating local landmarks and cultural elements to resonate with the target audience and generate excitement on social media.

Task: Designing branded content

Developing branded content graphics for social media posts

Example Prompt 1:
Create a series of social media graphics that incorporate our brand colors and logo, while also highlighting key product features or benefits.

Example Prompt 2:
Design a set of branded content templates for Instagram and Facebook posts, including variations for different types of content such as quotes, promotions, and announcements.

Example Prompt 3:
Develop a cohesive visual theme for our social media presence,

including custom graphics for cover photos, profile pictures, and story highlights that reflect our brand identity.

Example Prompt 4:
Produce a collection of branded content graphics that can be used across multiple platforms, ensuring consistency in style and messaging while catering to the unique requirements of each platform.

Task: Designing interactive graphics

Creating engaging and interactive graphics for social media posts

Example Prompt 1:
Design an interactive infographic that visually explains a complex concept or process in a simple and engaging way.

Example Prompt 2:
Create a series of interactive social media posts that encourage user engagement through polls, quizzes, or interactive elements.

Example Prompt 3:
Develop a visually appealing and interactive timeline graphic to showcase the evolution of a product, brand, or industry trend.

Example Prompt 4:
Design an interactive map graphic that allows users to explore different locations, events, or data points related to a specific topic or theme.

Task: Designing animated graphics

Developing animated graphics for social media posts

Example Prompt 1:
Create an animated graphic that showcases a product or service in a visually engaging way for a social media post.

Example Prompt 2:

Design an animated graphic that conveys a specific message or call-to-action for a social media campaign.

Example Prompt 3:
Develop an animated graphic that incorporates brand elements and colors to maintain consistency across social media posts.

Example Prompt 4:
Produce an animated graphic that highlights a special promotion or event for use in a social media post.

Task: Designing carousel posts

Crafting visually appealing carousel posts for social media platforms

Example Prompt 1:
Create a carousel post series that showcases the evolution of a product or service, using a combination of images, graphics, and text to tell a compelling visual story.

Example Prompt 2:
Design a carousel post set that highlights different features or benefits of a product, using a cohesive color scheme and layout to maintain visual consistency.

Example Prompt 3:
Craft a carousel post sequence that educates and engages the audience on a specific topic or industry trend, using a mix of infographics, illustrations, and photographs to convey information in an eye-catching way.

Example Prompt 4:
Develop a carousel post series that promotes a special event or campaign, incorporating dynamic visuals and persuasive messaging to drive audience participation and excitement.

Idea: Infographics for social media

ChatGPT can help generate data-driven content and statistics to create visually appealing infographics for social media platforms.

Example Prompt 1:
Create an infographic showcasing the impact of social media on mental health, using data and statistics provided by ChatGPT to highlight the prevalence of anxiety and depression among social media users.

Example Prompt 2:
Design an infographic illustrating the growth of e-commerce sales through social media platforms, utilizing ChatGPT's data-driven insights to showcase the increasing trend of online shopping and consumer behavior.

Example Prompt 3:
Develop an infographic highlighting the most popular social media platforms among different age groups, using ChatGPT's statistical analysis to visually represent the demographic usage and engagement on various social media channels.

Example Prompt 4:
Produce an infographic demonstrating the effectiveness of influencer marketing on social media, incorporating ChatGPT's data and statistics to showcase the impact of influencer collaborations on brand awareness and consumer engagement.

Idea: Quote graphics

ChatGPT can assist in generating relevant and engaging quotes to be used in social media graphics.

Example Prompt 1:
Create a series of visually appealing quote graphics using ChatGPT-generated quotes that resonate with our brand's values and messaging.

Example Prompt 2:

Design quote graphics for our social media channels using ChatGPT-suggested quotes that align with our current marketing campaign.

Example Prompt 3:
Utilize ChatGPT's assistance to curate impactful quotes and transform them into eye-catching graphics for our upcoming social media content calendar.

Example Prompt 4:
Collaborate with ChatGPT to produce quote graphics that capture the essence of our brand and resonate with our target audience, enhancing our social media presence.

Idea: Interactive social media posts

ChatGPT can help brainstorm and generate ideas for interactive social media posts such as polls, quizzes, and interactive graphics.

Example Prompt 1:
Hey ChatGPT, I need help brainstorming ideas for interactive social media posts. Can you suggest some engaging poll questions or quiz topics that would resonate with my audience?

Example Prompt 2:
ChatGPT, I'm looking to create interactive graphics for my social media posts. Can you help me come up with some visually appealing and interactive design concepts that will grab attention and encourage engagement?

Example Prompt 3:
I want to spice up my social media content with interactive elements. ChatGPT, can you assist me in generating ideas for interactive posts that will encourage my followers to participate and interact with my brand?

Example Prompt 4:
ChatGPT, I'm in need of fresh ideas for interactive social media

posts. Can you help me brainstorm and develop concepts for interactive content that will captivate my audience and drive engagement on my social media platforms?

Idea: Animated social media graphics

ChatGPT can provide ideas and concepts for animated graphics to make social media posts more engaging.

Example Prompt 1:
Can you provide concepts for animated social media graphics that would be eye-catching and shareable for a fitness brand's Instagram account?

Example Prompt 2:
I need ideas for animated graphics that can be used to promote a new product launch on Twitter. Can you help brainstorm some concepts?

Example Prompt 3:
I'm looking for creative concepts for animated social media graphics to promote a music event on Facebook. Can you provide some ideas that will stand out and capture attention?

Example Prompt 4:
I want to create engaging animated graphics for a food and beverage company's Pinterest page. Can you help generate concepts that will resonate with our audience?

Idea: Branded social media templates

ChatGPT can assist in creating branded templates for social media posts to maintain consistency in design.

Example Prompt 1:
Create a set of branded social media templates for our company's Instagram, Facebook, and Twitter accounts. Ensure that the design elements align with our brand guidelines and incorporate our logo and color scheme.

Example Prompt 2:
Design a series of customizable social media templates that can be easily edited for different promotions, events, and announcements. The templates should reflect our brand identity and maintain a cohesive look across all platforms.

Example Prompt 3:
Develop a collection of eye-catching social media templates that can be used for various types of content, such as quotes, product features, and announcements. The templates should be versatile and adaptable to different types of posts while staying true to our brand aesthetic.

Example Prompt 4:
Assist in creating a consistent visual identity for our social media presence by designing a set of branded templates for posts, stories, and cover images. The templates should reflect our brand's personality and values while maintaining a professional and polished appearance.

Idea: Storytelling through graphics

ChatGPT can help in brainstorming and creating graphics that tell a story or convey a message effectively on social media.

Example Prompt 1:
Prompt: "Create a series of graphics that visually narrate a short story or convey a specific message. Use ChatGPT to brainstorm ideas for the storyline and collaborate on the visual elements to effectively communicate the narrative on social media platforms."

Example Prompt 2:
Prompt: "Design a set of graphics that tell a sequential story or convey a message in a visually engaging way. Utilize ChatGPT to generate ideas for the plot and collaborate on the design elements to ensure the graphics effectively communicate the intended story or message on social media."

Example Prompt 3:

Prompt: *"Develop a collection of graphics that effectively convey a story or message through visual storytelling. Leverage ChatGPT to brainstorm creative concepts for the narrative and collaborate on the design elements to ensure the graphics effectively communicate the intended story or message on social media platforms."*

Example Prompt 4:

Prompt: *"Produce a series of graphics that effectively tell a story or convey a message through visual storytelling. Use ChatGPT to generate ideas for the narrative and collaborate on the design elements to ensure the graphics effectively communicate the intended story or message on social media."*

Idea: Data visualization graphics

ChatGPT can support in creating visually appealing graphics to represent data and statistics for social media posts.

Example Prompt 1:

Create a visually engaging infographic representing the latest social media engagement statistics for our company's accounts. Include key metrics such as likes, shares, and comments in a visually appealing format.

Example Prompt 2:

Design a series of bar graphs and pie charts to showcase the demographic breakdown of our social media followers. Use color and typography to make the data easy to understand and visually appealing.

Example Prompt 3:

Develop a set of data visualization graphics to illustrate the growth of our social media following over the past year. Incorporate line graphs and trend lines to highlight our progress.

Example Prompt 4:

Design a visually stunning graphic to showcase the impact of our recent social media campaign, including metrics such as reach, engagement, and conversion rates. Use creative visuals to make the data stand out on social media platforms.

Idea: Event promotion graphics

ChatGPT can assist in generating ideas and designs for promoting events through social media graphics.

Example Prompt 1:
Create a series of eye-catching social media graphics to promote a music festival happening in a local city. Incorporate elements of music, excitement, and the city's skyline to capture the attention of potential attendees.

Example Prompt 2:
Design a set of visually appealing graphics to promote a charity gala event, highlighting the cause and the impact of the event. Use colors and imagery that convey a sense of elegance and philanthropy to attract donors and supporters.

Example Prompt 3:
Develop a collection of vibrant and engaging graphics to promote a food and wine festival, showcasing the variety of culinary experiences and the picturesque vineyard setting. Use mouth-watering imagery and playful typography to entice food and wine enthusiasts.

Example Prompt 4:
Craft a series of dynamic social media graphics to promote a fitness and wellness expo, emphasizing the energy, vitality, and diversity of activities available at the event. Incorporate images of people in action, along with motivational quotes and bold typography to inspire participation.

Idea: Product showcase graphics

ChatGPT can help in creating graphics to showcase products or services effectively on social media platforms.

Example Prompt 1:
Create a series of eye-catching graphics to showcase our latest product line on Instagram, highlighting key features and benefits in a visually appealing way.

Example Prompt 2:
Design a set of promotional graphics for our upcoming service launch, incorporating our brand colors and logo to maintain a cohesive look across all social media platforms.

Example Prompt 3:
Develop a visually engaging infographic to showcase the benefits of our new subscription service, using compelling visuals and concise text to capture the attention of potential customers.

Example Prompt 4:
Produce a series of product showcase graphics for our website, featuring high-quality images and persuasive copy to effectively communicate the value of our offerings to visitors.

Idea: Social media ad graphics

ChatGPT can provide ideas and concepts for creating effective ad graphics for social media advertising campaigns.

Example Prompt 1:
Hey ChatGPT, I need some fresh ideas for creating eye-catching ad graphics for a social media campaign promoting our new product. Can you help me brainstorm some concepts and designs that will grab attention and drive engagement?

Example Prompt 2:
ChatGPT, I'm looking to revamp our social media ad graphics to better align with our brand and messaging. Can you provide some creative concepts and design suggestions that will help us stand out and connect with our target audience?

Example Prompt 3:
I'm in need of some inspiration for creating visually appealing ad graphics for an upcoming social media advertising campaign. ChatGPT, can you assist me in generating ideas and concepts that will resonate with our audience and drive conversions?

Example Prompt 4:
ChatGPT, I'm struggling to come up with compelling ad graphics for our social media advertising efforts. Can you provide some innovative design concepts and suggestions that will help us effectively communicate our message and drive results?

Idea: Seasonal/holiday-themed graphics

ChatGPT can support in brainstorming and creating graphics for seasonal or holiday-themed social media posts.

Example Prompt 1:
Create a series of festive graphics for an upcoming holiday campaign, incorporating traditional symbols and colors associated with the holiday.

Example Prompt 2:
Brainstorm and design a set of seasonal graphics for an upcoming social media calendar, including themes for spring, summer, fall, and winter.

Example Prompt 3:
Develop a collection of holiday-themed graphics for a special promotion or event, incorporating elements such as snowflakes, holly, and seasonal greetings.

Example Prompt 4:
Collaborate on creating eye-catching graphics for a series of seasonal sales and promotions, utilizing vibrant colors and playful imagery to capture the spirit of the holiday season.

Idea: User-generated content graphics

ChatGPT can assist in creating graphics using user-generated content to promote engagement on social media platforms.

Example Prompt 1:
Prompt: "Hey ChatGPT, can you help me create engaging graphics for social media using user-generated content? I want to showcase the creativity of our community and promote engagement on our platforms."

Example Prompt 2:
Prompt: "ChatGPT, I need your assistance in designing graphics that incorporate user-generated content to drive interaction on our social media channels. Can you help me with this?"

Example Prompt 3:
Prompt: "I'm looking to create visually appealing graphics for social media that feature user-generated content. ChatGPT, can you support me in this endeavor to boost engagement and showcase our community's contributions?"

Example Prompt 4:
Prompt: "ChatGPT, I'm seeking your expertise in utilizing user-generated content to craft compelling graphics for our social media presence. Can you assist me in creating visually captivating designs that will encourage interaction and participation from our audience?"

ANIMATION BASICS

BRINGING DESIGNS TO LIFE: INTRODUCTION TO ANIMATION

In the ever-evolving world of graphic design, animation has become an essential tool for creating captivating motion graphics. This chapter will delve into the fundamental principles and techniques of animation, offering valuable insights to graphic designers who aim to master this dynamic art form.

Let's follow the journey of Alex, a talented graphic designer seeking to expand his skill set into animation. With the guidance of AI-driven tools like ChatGPT, he embarks on this creative adventure.

Principle 1: Timing and Spacing

One of the core principles of animation is timing and spacing. It's about controlling the speed and rhythm of movement to create a natural and engaging flow. ChatGPT advises Alex to start with a clear understanding of the desired animation duration and the number of frames required.

Principle 2: Ease In and Ease Out

ChatGPT emphasizes the importance of easing in and easing out. This technique involves gradually accelerating and decelerating an object's movement. It adds a sense of realism and weight to animations. Alex experiments with this concept, ensuring his animations feel more lifelike.

Principle 3: Anticipation and Follow-Through

Anticipation and follow-through are essential for creating fluid animations. ChatGPT encourages Alex to consider how objects prepare for movement and how they settle afterward. This helps convey a sense of purpose and intention in his animations.

Principle 4: Squash and Stretch

Squash and stretch is a classic animation technique that adds flexibility and vitality to objects. ChatGPT suggests that Alex uses this principle to give his animations a dynamic and visually appealing quality.

Principle 5: Arcs and Paths

Creating animations that follow natural paths and arcs is crucial for realism. ChatGPT advises Alex to envision the trajectory of an object's movement and to ensure that it flows naturally within the animation.

Principle 6: Secondary Motion

Secondary motion adds depth and complexity to animations. It involves animating additional elements to complement the primary motion. ChatGPT recommends that Alex experiments with secondary motion to create more engaging and lifelike animations.

Principle 7: Staging

Staging is about presenting the animation in a way that guides the viewer's attention effectively. ChatGPT encourages Alex to consider the composition, framing, and focal points within his animations to ensure clarity and impact.

As Alex continues his journey into animation, he finds that these principles and techniques, combined with the assistance of AI-driven tools, empower him to create compelling motion graphics. With each project, his skills in animation grow, and he gains confidence in his ability to captivate audiences through dynamic visuals.

In conclusion, animation is a powerful medium for graphic designers to convey their messages and engage their audiences. By mastering these fundamental principles and techniques, and with the support of AI tools like ChatGPT, graphic designers like Alex can breathe life into their designs and elevate their creative capabilities. Embrace the world of animation, and watch your designs come to life with motion, emotion, and impact.

Note: For the strategies, tasks, and ideas outlined in this chapter, consider harnessing AI to produce the necessary images. Explore my video training on: jeroenerne.com/AI-images for comprehensive guidance.

Task: Keyframe animation

ChatGPT can help explain the concept of keyframe animation and provide examples.

Example Prompt 1:
Can you explain the concept of keyframe animation and how it is used in graphic design and animation?

Example Prompt 2:
What are some common software tools used for creating keyframe animations, and how do they work?

Example Prompt 3:
Can you provide examples of keyframe animations in popular movies or video games, and explain how they were created?

Example Prompt 4:
How can keyframe animation be used to create dynamic and engaging visual content for websites or social media platforms?

Task: Timing and spacing

ChatGPT can provide tips and best practices for timing and spacing in animation.

Example Prompt 1:
Can you provide some tips for creating smooth and natural timing and spacing in animation? What are some common mistakes to avoid?

Example Prompt 2:
How can I use ChatGPT to improve the timing and spacing of my animated sequences? Are there any specific techniques or tools I should be aware of?

Example Prompt 3:
What are some best practices for adjusting timing and spacing in different types of animations, such as character movements or special effects? How can ChatGPT help me with this?

Example Prompt 4:
I'm struggling with getting the timing and spacing just right in my animations. Can ChatGPT suggest some resources or examples to help me improve in this area?

Task: Easing

ChatGPT can explain different easing functions and how to use them in animation.

Example Prompt 1:
Can you explain the concept of easing in animation and provide examples of different easing functions?

Example Prompt 2:
How can easing functions enhance the visual appeal of an animated graphic or design?

Example Prompt 3:
What are some best practices for incorporating easing functions into graphic design and animation?

Example Prompt 4:
Can you walk me through the process of applying easing functions to a specific animation or design project?

Task: Motion paths

ChatGPT can provide examples and explanations of how to

create and use motion paths in animation.

Example Prompt 1:
Can you provide a step-by-step guide on how to create motion paths in Adobe After Effects for a simple animation?

Example Prompt 2:
I'm looking for examples of how to use motion paths to create smooth and realistic movement in 2D character animations. Can you help with that?

Example Prompt 3:
I'm interested in learning how to use motion paths in graphic design software like Procreate for creating animated illustrations. Can you demonstrate some techniques?

Example Prompt 4:
Could you explain the concept of easing in and easing out when using motion paths in animation, and provide some practical examples of how to achieve this effect?

Task: Character animation

ChatGPT can provide tips and techniques for creating character animations.

Example Prompt 1:
Can you provide tips for creating smooth and fluid character animations, especially for complex movements like running or jumping?

Example Prompt 2:
What are some techniques for adding personality and emotion to character animations, such as facial expressions and body language?

Example Prompt 3:
I'm struggling with creating realistic and natural movements for my character animations. Can you suggest some resources or

tutorials to improve my skills in this area?

Example Prompt 4:
How can I use principles of graphic design to enhance the visual appeal of my character animations, such as color theory and composition?

Task: Effects animation

ChatGPT can explain how to create various effects such as explosions, smoke, and fire in animation.

Example Prompt 1:
Can you explain the process of creating a realistic explosion effect in animation, including the use of particle systems and lighting techniques?

Example Prompt 2:
How can I achieve a convincing smoke effect in my animation, and what are some key principles to keep in mind when animating smoke dynamics?

Example Prompt 3:
I'm interested in learning how to animate fire effects that look natural and dynamic. Can you provide tips on creating realistic fire movement and color variation?

Example Prompt 4:
What are some advanced techniques for adding impact and shockwave effects to an explosion animation, and how can I make them look more dynamic and impactful?

Task: Lip sync

ChatGPT can provide guidance on how to achieve realistic lip sync in character animation.

Example Prompt 1:
How can I use ChatGPT to improve the lip sync in my character

animation? Can you provide tips on matching the lip movements to the dialogue?

Example Prompt 2:
I'm struggling to make my character's lip movements look realistic in my animation. Can ChatGPT help me understand the nuances of lip sync and provide guidance on achieving a more natural look?

Example Prompt 3:
I want to create more convincing lip sync in my character animation. Can ChatGPT suggest techniques or resources to help me improve this aspect of my work?

Example Prompt 4:
As a graphic designer, I'm looking for ways to enhance the lip sync in my character animations. Can ChatGPT offer insights or best practices for achieving more accurate and lifelike lip movements?

Task: 3D animation basics

ChatGPT can explain the basics of 3D animation and provide examples.

Example Prompt 1:
Can you explain the concept of keyframes in 3D animation and how they are used to create movement in a scene?

Example Prompt 2:
What are some common techniques for creating realistic lighting and shadows in 3D animation, and how do they contribute to the overall visual appeal of a scene?

Example Prompt 3:
Could you provide an example of how 3D animation is used in the film industry to enhance storytelling and create immersive visual experiences for audiences?

Example Prompt 4:
How do 3D animators use rigging and character modeling to bring

life and personality to their creations, and what are some best practices for achieving realistic movement and expressions?

Task: Camera animation

ChatGPT can provide tips and techniques for animating the camera in a scene.

Example Prompt 1:
Can you provide tips for creating smooth camera movements in a 3D animation scene?

Example Prompt 2:
How can I use ChatGPT to learn about different camera angles and their effects on storytelling in animation?

Example Prompt 3:
What are some techniques for creating dynamic camera movements to enhance the visual impact of a scene?

Example Prompt 4:
Can ChatGPT help me understand the principles of camera animation, such as easing in and out, and how to apply them in my projects?

Task: Rendering

ChatGPT can explain the rendering process and provide tips for optimizing rendering settings.

Example Prompt 1:
Can you explain the rendering process in graphic design and how it differs from other design processes?

Example Prompt 2:
What are some common challenges in rendering and how can they be overcome?

Example Prompt 3:
What are some tips for optimizing rendering settings to achieve the

best results in graphic design projects?

Example Prompt 4:
Can you provide examples of how different rendering settings can impact the final outcome of a design project?

Idea: Animated logo design

Create a dynamic and engaging version of a company's logo for use in videos and on websites.

Example Prompt 1:
ChatGPT, I need your help to create an animated logo design for a tech startup. The logo should be dynamic and engaging, suitable for use in promotional videos and on the company's website. Can you assist with this project?

Example Prompt 2:
As a graphic designer, I'm looking to create a captivating animated version of a company's logo for their upcoming marketing campaign. ChatGPT, can you provide support in developing a visually appealing and dynamic logo animation for this purpose?

Example Prompt 3:
I'm in need of a unique animated logo design for a client's fashion brand. The logo should be eye-catching and suitable for use in online advertisements and social media. ChatGPT, can you help me bring this vision to life?

Example Prompt 4:
ChatGPT, I'm seeking assistance in creating an animated version of a company's logo for their new product launch. The animation should be modern and engaging, perfect for showcasing on their website and in promotional videos. Can you support me in this project as a graphic designer?

Idea: Explainer video animation

Produce animated videos to explain complex concepts or

products in a visually appealing way.

Example Prompt 1:
Prompt: "Create a 2-minute animated video explaining the concept of blockchain technology in a visually engaging and easy-to-understand manner."

Example Prompt 2:
Prompt: "Produce a series of animated videos to explain the features and benefits of our new software product, showcasing its functionality in an engaging and visually appealing way."

Example Prompt 3:
Prompt: "Design an animated video to simplify the process of understanding the principles of sustainable energy, using visually captivating graphics and clear explanations."

Example Prompt 4:
Prompt: "Develop an animated video to illustrate the intricate workings of artificial intelligence, presenting complex algorithms and processes in a visually stimulating and easy-to-follow format."

Idea: Character animation

Develop animated characters for use in marketing materials, social media, or brand storytelling.

Example Prompt 1:
Create a series of animated characters that can be used in marketing materials to promote our brand's products and services. These characters should be versatile and able to convey different emotions and actions to engage our audience.

Example Prompt 2:
Design a set of animated characters that can be used across our social media platforms to tell a visual story about our brand and its values. These characters should be relatable and memorable to leave a lasting impression on our audience.

Example Prompt 3:

Develop a collection of animated characters that can be integrated into our brand's storytelling efforts, whether through short videos, GIFs, or interactive content. These characters should embody our brand's personality and resonate with our target audience.

Example Prompt 4:

Create a library of animated characters that can be easily customized and adapted for various marketing materials, allowing us to maintain a consistent visual identity across different channels. These characters should be adaptable to different scenarios and messaging while staying true to our brand's image.

Idea: Motion graphics

Create visually appealing and dynamic graphics for use in videos, presentations, and websites.

Example Prompt 1:

Create a 15-second motion graphic animation to be used as an intro for a YouTube video series on technology trends.

Example Prompt 2:

Design a set of dynamic graphics to be used in a presentation for a new product launch, including animated charts and visual representations of data.

Example Prompt 3:

Develop a series of visually appealing motion graphics for a website homepage, including animated banners and interactive elements to engage visitors.

Example Prompt 4:

Produce a motion graphic video to showcase the features and benefits of a new mobile app, including dynamic transitions and engaging visual effects.

Idea: Animated infographics

Turn static infographics into engaging and interactive animated visuals.

Example Prompt 1:
Create a dynamic and visually appealing animation of the static infographic provided, adding movement and interactivity to engage the audience.

Example Prompt 2:
Design an animated infographic that effectively communicates the data and information from the static infographic, using creative visuals and interactive elements.

Example Prompt 3:
Transform the existing static infographic into an animated and interactive format, enhancing the storytelling and engagement through motion graphics and interactive features.

Example Prompt 4:
Produce an animated version of the static infographic, incorporating engaging animations and interactive elements to bring the data and information to life in a visually compelling way.

Idea: Animated social media posts

Design animated content for social media platforms to increase engagement and brand awareness.

Example Prompt 1:
Create a series of animated social media posts for our brand's upcoming product launch, showcasing its features and benefits in a visually engaging way.

Example Prompt 2:
Design eye-catching animated content for our social media

platforms to promote our upcoming event and drive attendance.

Example Prompt 3:
Develop a set of animated social media posts to highlight customer testimonials and success stories, showcasing the impact of our products/services.

Example Prompt 4:
Produce animated content for our social media channels to celebrate special occasions and holidays, engaging our audience and fostering a sense of community.

Idea: Animated website elements

Incorporate animated elements into website design to enhance user experience and visual appeal.

Example Prompt 1:
Create a series of animated call-to-action buttons and banners to grab the attention of website visitors and encourage interaction with key features or promotions.

Example Prompt 2:
Design animated background elements such as subtle moving patterns or textures to add depth and visual interest to the website without distracting from the content.

Example Prompt 3:
Develop animated transitions and effects for page navigation, creating a seamless and engaging user experience as visitors move through different sections of the website.

Example Prompt 4:
Integrate animated illustrations or icons that visually represent key concepts or features, adding a dynamic and interactive element to the website's overall design.

Idea: Animated product demonstrations

Create animated videos to showcase the features and benefits of a product or service.

Example Prompt 1:
ChatGPT, I need your help to create an animated product demonstration video for our new software product. Please generate a script and storyboard for a 2-minute video that highlights the key features and benefits of the software.

Example Prompt 2:
ChatGPT, as a graphic designer, I need your assistance in creating an animated video to showcase the functionality of our new mobile app. Can you help me by providing a visual concept and animation ideas for a 1-minute promotional video?

Example Prompt 3:
ChatGPT, I'm looking to create an animated product demonstration video for our latest consumer electronics product. Can you help me by generating a series of animated scenes that effectively communicate the unique features and advantages of the product?

Example Prompt 4:
ChatGPT, I need your support in developing an animated video to demonstrate the benefits of our new subscription-based service. Please assist me in creating a visually engaging and informative animation that effectively communicates the value proposition of our service.

Idea: Interactive animations

Develop interactive animations for use in presentations, websites, or digital marketing campaigns.

Example Prompt 1:
Create a series of interactive animations that can be embedded into a website to engage visitors and enhance user experience.

Example Prompt 2:

Design interactive animations that can be used in digital marketing campaigns to capture audience attention and increase brand awareness.

Example Prompt 3:
Develop interactive animations that can be integrated into presentations to make them more engaging and visually appealing.

Example Prompt 4:
Produce a set of interactive animations that can be customized and used across various platforms to create a cohesive and dynamic brand image.

Idea: Animated email marketing campaigns

Design animated visuals for email marketing campaigns to increase open and click-through rates.

Example Prompt 1:
Create a series of animated visuals that can be used in email marketing campaigns to grab the attention of subscribers and increase open rates. Consider incorporating eye-catching graphics and subtle motion to engage the audience.

Example Prompt 2:
Design animated email headers and banners that can be used to promote upcoming sales or events. The visuals should be attention-grabbing and encourage recipients to click through to learn more.

Example Prompt 3:
Develop a set of animated GIFs that can be embedded within email newsletters to showcase new products or services. The animations should be visually appealing and help drive click-through rates.

Example Prompt 4:
Produce animated visuals that tell a story or convey a message within the limited space of an email. These animations should be designed to captivate the audience and encourage them to take action, such as visiting a website or making a purchase.

Idea: Animated advertisements

Produce animated ads for use on digital platforms, TV, or in-store displays.

Example Prompt 1:
Create a series of animated advertisements for a new product launch, showcasing its features and benefits in a visually engaging way. These ads will be used across digital platforms, TV commercials, and in-store displays to maximize reach and impact.

Example Prompt 2:
Design a set of eye-catching animated ads to promote our upcoming sales event, incorporating dynamic visuals and compelling messaging to drive customer engagement and excitement. These ads will be utilized across various digital channels and in-store screens.

Example Prompt 3:
Develop a collection of animated advertisements to highlight our brand's unique selling points and key offerings, tailored for different target audiences and optimized for digital platforms, TV spots, and in-store displays. The ads should effectively communicate our brand identity and value proposition.

Example Prompt 4:
Produce a series of animated ads for our seasonal marketing campaign, featuring captivating visuals and persuasive storytelling to capture audience attention and drive sales. These ads will be deployed across digital platforms, TV commercials, and in-store displays to maximize brand visibility and impact.

Idea: Animated brand storytelling

Use animation to tell the story of a brand or company in a compelling and memorable way.

Example Prompt 1:

Create a 2-minute animated video that tells the origin story of our company, highlighting key milestones and achievements in a visually engaging way.

Example Prompt 2:

Design a series of animated characters that represent our brand values and ethos, and create a short animated story that showcases how these characters embody our brand identity.

Example Prompt 3:

Develop a storyboard for a 5-minute animated brand story that captures the essence of our company's mission, vision, and impact, using creative visuals and storytelling techniques.

Example Prompt 4:

Produce a 3-minute animated video that takes our audience on a journey through the evolution of our brand, from its inception to the present day, using captivating visuals and narrative elements.

PRINT PREPARATION AND FORMATS

FROM SCREEN TO PRINT: PREPARING YOUR DESIGNS

In the realm of graphic design, the transition from the digital canvas to the printed page demands precision and meticulous attention to detail. This chapter delves into the art of print preparation, shedding light on file formats, color profiles, and bleed settings – crucial elements that transform digital designs into tangible, eye-catching prints.

Let's journey alongside Emily, a seasoned graphic designer, as she navigates the complexities of preparing her latest project for print, armed with the support of AI, embodied by ChatGPT.

File Formats: The Foundation of Print

As Emily begins her print preparation, ChatGPT reminds her that selecting the right file format is paramount. For high-quality prints, she opts for formats like TIFF or PDF, which preserve image quality and maintain compatibility across various print platforms. The AI emphasizes the importance of maintaining layers and vectors when applicable, ensuring that the design retains its integrity during the printing process.

Color Profiles: A Spectrum of Accuracy

Emily understands that accurate color reproduction is critical in print. ChatGPT advises her to use CMYK color profiles for her designs, as they closely match the ink combinations used in the printing process. It highlights the importance of color calibration to ensure consistency between what's seen on screen and what emerges on paper.

Bleed Settings: Beyond the Edge

Emily encounters the concept of bleed settings, where ChatGPT steps in to clarify its significance. Bleed ensures that images or colors extend beyond the edge of the document, safeguarding against potential misalignment during printing. It's a crucial safeguard that ensures the final product looks as intended.

Print-Ready Check: A Final Assessment

As Emily nears the completion of her print preparation, ChatGPT recommends conducting a thorough print-ready check. This involves verifying resolution, fonts, and image placement. The AI encourages Emily to use preflight software to catch any potential issues before sending the design to the printer.

AI-Assisted Proofing: A Guardian of Quality

Before finalizing her print files, ChatGPT introduces Emily to AI-powered proofing tools that can automatically detect and correct common print-related issues. These tools help ensure that her designs meet the highest standards of print quality, saving her time and reducing the risk of errors.

With ChatGPT's guidance, Emily completes her print preparation with confidence. Her files are optimized for the printing press, color-accurate, and equipped with bleed settings that guarantee a seamless transition from screen to print. She understands that the synergy of human creativity and AI assistance ensures her designs are print-ready and poised for success.

In conclusion, print preparation is a meticulous endeavor that demands attention to detail and adherence to industry best practices. AI, represented by ChatGPT, proves to be an invaluable partner in this process. By understanding file formats, color profiles, bleed settings, and leveraging AI-assisted proofing, graphic designers like Emily can ensure their designs shine brightly on the printed page. Embrace the art of print preparation, and watch your creations come to life in vibrant, tangible form.

Task: File format conversion

Converting design files to different print-ready formats such as PDF, EPS, or AI.

Example Prompt 1:

Can you recommend a reliable tool or software for converting design files to PDF, EPS, or AI formats for print-ready purposes?

Example Prompt 2:
What are the best practices for ensuring a smooth and accurate conversion of design files to different print-ready formats such as PDF, EPS, or AI?

Example Prompt 3:
Are there any specific considerations or potential challenges to keep in mind when converting design files to PDF, EPS, or AI for print-ready use?

Example Prompt 4:
Can you provide step-by-step instructions or a tutorial on how to effectively convert design files to PDF, EPS, or AI formats for print-ready purposes?

Task: Color management

Ensuring accurate color reproduction and consistency across different print materials.

Example Prompt 1:
How can I ensure accurate color reproduction and consistency across different print materials, especially when working with a variety of printing methods and substrates?

Example Prompt 2:
What are some best practices for color management when designing for print, and how can I maintain consistency in color reproduction across different print materials?

Example Prompt 3:
Can you provide tips for calibrating monitors and printers to ensure accurate color reproduction in print materials, and how can I maintain consistency in color across different print materials?

Example Prompt 4:
What tools or software do you recommend for managing color and ensuring accurate color reproduction and consistency across

different print materials, and what are some common challenges to watch out for in color management for print design?

Task: Bleed and trim setup

Setting up proper bleed and trim marks for print production.

Example Prompt 1:
Can you provide step-by-step instructions for setting up bleed and trim marks in Adobe InDesign for print production?

Example Prompt 2:
What are the standard bleed and trim measurements for a typical print project, and how can I ensure my design meets these requirements?

Example Prompt 3:
Are there any specific considerations or best practices for setting up bleed and trim marks for different types of print materials, such as business cards, brochures, or posters?

Example Prompt 4:
Can you recommend any online resources or tutorials for learning more about bleed and trim setup and print production in graphic design?

Task: Image resolution optimization

Adjusting image resolution for optimal print quality.

Example Prompt 1:
How can I optimize the resolution of my images for high-quality printing?

Example Prompt 2:
What are the best practices for adjusting image resolution to ensure optimal print quality?

Example Prompt 3:
Can you provide tips for optimizing image resolution for different

print sizes and formats?

Example Prompt 4:
What tools or software do you recommend for adjusting image resolution for optimal print quality?

Task: Font management

Ensuring all fonts are embedded or outlined for print compatibility.

Example Prompt 1:
Can you recommend a font management software or tool that ensures all fonts are embedded or outlined for print compatibility?

Example Prompt 2:
What are some best practices for embedding or outlining fonts to ensure print compatibility in graphic design projects?

Example Prompt 3:
How can I check if all fonts are properly embedded or outlined in my design files before sending them for print?

Example Prompt 4:
Are there any specific considerations or tips for managing fonts and ensuring print compatibility in different design software or platforms?

Task: Print proofing

Reviewing digital proofs for accuracy before finalizing print files.

Example Prompt 1:
Can you help me review this digital proof for accuracy before I send it to print?

Example Prompt 2:
I need assistance with print proofing this design to ensure it meets all necessary specifications.

Example Prompt 3:
I'm looking for feedback on this digital proof to ensure it's ready for finalizing and printing.

Example Prompt 4:
I need a second set of eyes to review this print file for any errors or inaccuracies before it goes to print.

Task: Print specifications compliance

Ensuring designs meet the specific requirements of the chosen printing method and materials.

Example Prompt 1:
Can you ensure that the design is in CMYK color mode and at least 300 DPI for optimal print quality?

Example Prompt 2:
Please double-check that all fonts are outlined or embedded to avoid any potential issues with printing.

Example Prompt 3:
Are there any specific bleed and trim requirements we need to consider for this design?

Example Prompt 4:
Have you confirmed that the design meets the file format and size specifications for the chosen printing method and materials?

Task: Packaging design setup

Preparing print files for packaging materials with appropriate die lines and folding guides.

Example Prompt 1:
Can you provide me with a chatGPT prompt for setting up packaging design with appropriate die lines and folding guides for a box packaging?

Example Prompt 2:
I need assistance in creating print files for packaging materials using chatGPT, including die lines and folding guides. Can you help me with a prompt for this?

Example Prompt 3:
Looking for a chatGPT prompt to guide me in preparing print files for packaging materials, ensuring proper die lines and folding guides are included for the packaging design setup.

Example Prompt 4:
Seeking a chatGPT prompt to help me with the technical aspects of packaging design, specifically in setting up print files with die lines and folding guides for packaging materials.

Task: Variable data printing setup

Setting up print files to accommodate variable data elements such as personalized text or images.

Example Prompt 1:
How can I optimize my print files to accommodate variable data elements such as personalized text or images for a direct mail campaign?

Example Prompt 2:
What are the best practices for setting up print files for variable data printing to ensure accurate and consistent results?

Example Prompt 3:
Can you provide tips for incorporating variable data elements into my print design while maintaining a cohesive and visually appealing layout?

Example Prompt 4:
I'm looking to streamline my variable data printing setup process - what software or tools do you recommend for efficiently managing personalized print files?

Task: Print file organization

Organizing print files and assets for efficient handoff to printers or production teams.

Example Prompt 1:
Can you provide a step-by-step guide on how to organize print files for efficient handoff to printers? What are the best practices for file naming and folder structure?

Example Prompt 2:
What are some common mistakes to avoid when organizing print files and assets for production teams? How can we ensure that all necessary files are included and easily accessible?

Example Prompt 3:
Can you share any tips or tools for managing version control and file revisions when working with print files? How can we streamline the process of updating and tracking changes?

Example Prompt 4:
What are the key considerations for preparing print files for different types of printing processes (e.g. offset, digital, large format)? How can we optimize file organization to accommodate these variations?

Idea: Print-ready file checklist

A checklist of all the necessary elements to ensure a file is print-ready, including bleed, resolution, and color mode.

Example Prompt 1:
Create a comprehensive checklist for print-ready files, including specifications for bleed, resolution, and color mode. Provide detailed explanations for each item on the checklist to ensure clarity for designers and print professionals.

Example Prompt 2:

Design a visually appealing infographic that outlines the essential elements of a print-ready file checklist. Include clear visuals and concise descriptions to help designers understand and implement the necessary requirements for print preparation.

Example Prompt 3:

Develop a printable PDF guide that walks designers through the process of ensuring their files are print-ready. Include step-by-step instructions, visual examples, and tips for troubleshooting common issues to support designers in creating high-quality print materials.

Example Prompt 4:

Produce a series of social media graphics that highlight key components of a print-ready file checklist, such as bleed, resolution, and color mode. Create engaging visuals and concise captions to educate and remind designers of the important considerations for print preparation.

Idea: Standard print formats guide

A guide to standard print formats for various materials such as business cards, brochures, and posters.

Example Prompt 1:

Can you create a visually appealing and informative infographic that outlines the standard print formats for business cards, brochures, and posters? Include dimensions, bleed areas, and any other important design considerations.

Example Prompt 2:

Design a series of templates for business cards, brochures, and posters that adhere to standard print formats. Provide options for different styles and layouts to accommodate various design preferences.

Example Prompt 3:

Develop a comprehensive guide that explains the importance of standard print formats for different materials and provides tips for optimizing designs within these parameters. Include visual examples and practical advice for designers.

Example Prompt 4:
Produce a set of visually engaging and easy-to-understand illustrations that demonstrate the proper layout and dimensions for standard print formats of business cards, brochures, and posters. These illustrations should serve as a quick reference for designers and printers.

Idea: Print file templates
Pre-made templates for common print materials in various sizes and formats.

Example Prompt 1:
Create a set of pre-made templates for business cards, including standard sizes and bleed areas, in both horizontal and vertical orientations.

Example Prompt 2:
Design templates for flyers in various sizes, such as letter, A4, and tabloid, with options for single or double-sided layouts.

Example Prompt 3:
Develop print file templates for posters in standard sizes like 11x17, 18x24, and 24x36, with options for both portrait and landscape orientations.

Example Prompt 4:
Produce pre-made templates for brochures, including tri-fold and bi-fold layouts, with designated areas for images, text, and branding elements.

Idea: Color management tips
Tips for managing color profiles and ensuring accurate color reproduction in print.

Example Prompt 1:
Can you provide a step-by-step guide on how to calibrate monitors for accurate color reproduction in graphic design projects?

Example Prompt 2:
Please share best practices for choosing and using color profiles in Adobe Creative Suite to ensure consistent color across different devices and print materials.

Example Prompt 3:
I'm looking for tips on how to adjust color settings for different printing processes (CMYK, Pantone, etc.) to achieve accurate color reproduction. Can you help with that?

Example Prompt 4:
Could you provide insights on how to troubleshoot common color management issues in graphic design, such as color shifts and inconsistencies in printed materials?

Idea: File compression techniques

Techniques for compressing print files without sacrificing quality for easier sharing and printing.

Example Prompt 1:
Can you provide a detailed explanation of the various file compression techniques that can be used to reduce the size of print files without compromising the quality of the images and text?

Example Prompt 2:
Please outline the best practices for compressing print files in a way that allows for easier sharing and printing, while maintaining the integrity of the original design and layout.

Example Prompt 3:
I need guidance on how to effectively compress print files for efficient storage and transfer, while ensuring that the final output maintains high resolution and clarity. Can you assist with this?

Example Prompt 4:
Could you offer insights into the most effective methods for compressing print files without sacrificing the quality of the images and text, in order to facilitate seamless sharing and printing processes?

Idea: Print file proofing checklist

A checklist for proofing print files to catch any potential issues before sending them to print.

Example Prompt 1:
Create a comprehensive checklist for proofing print files, including items such as color accuracy, image resolution, and bleed margins, to ensure high-quality print results.

Example Prompt 2:
Design a visually appealing and easy-to-follow print file proofing checklist that can be easily printed and used by graphic designers and print professionals.

Example Prompt 3:
Develop a digital interactive version of a print file proofing checklist that allows users to check off items and make notes directly within the document for efficient collaboration and communication.

Example Prompt 4:
Produce a series of visual examples and explanations to accompany the print file proofing checklist, demonstrating common print file issues and how to identify and address them effectively.

Idea: Print file optimization guide

A guide to optimizing print files for different printing methods and materials.

Example Prompt 1:

Can you provide a step-by-step guide on optimizing print files for various printing methods such as offset, digital, and screen printing? Include tips on color management, resolution, and file formats for each method.

Example Prompt 2:

I need a comprehensive guide on optimizing print files for different materials like paper, fabric, and plastic. Please cover topics such as bleed, trim, and safety margins for each material.

Example Prompt 3:

Could you create a visual infographic that explains the best practices for print file optimization, including examples of properly optimized files for different printing methods and materials?

Example Prompt 4:

I'm looking for a tutorial video on print file optimization, specifically focusing on how to adjust file settings for optimal printing results. Can you provide a detailed walkthrough with practical examples?

Idea: Print file troubleshooting tips

Tips for troubleshooting common issues that arise when preparing print files, such as pixelation or incorrect color rendering.

Example Prompt 1:

ChatGPT, can you provide a step-by-step guide for troubleshooting pixelation issues in print files? Include tips for adjusting image resolution and file formats to ensure high-quality printing.

Example Prompt 2:

I need assistance with troubleshooting color rendering problems in print files. Can you provide tips for adjusting color profiles and ensuring accurate color representation in the final printed output?

Example Prompt 3:

ChatGPT, I'm encountering issues with print file formatting. Can you help me troubleshoot common formatting errors and provide tips for optimizing print file layouts for professional printing?

Example Prompt 4:

I'm looking for guidance on troubleshooting common print file issues such as bleed and trim errors. Can you provide tips for adjusting file dimensions and ensuring proper margins for print-ready files?

Idea: Print file export settings

Recommended export settings for various print file formats, such as PDF or EPS.

Example Prompt 1:

As a Graphic Designer, I need ChatGPT to provide me with the recommended export settings for PDF files for high-quality print. Please include details on color mode, resolution, and compression options.

Example Prompt 2:

Can ChatGPT assist me in understanding the best export settings for EPS files for print production? I need information on maintaining vector quality, color profiles, and compatibility with different design software.

Example Prompt 3:

I'm looking for guidance on the optimal export settings for CMYK and spot color printing in PDF format. Can ChatGPT provide me with a comprehensive breakdown of settings for both types of printing?

Example Prompt 4:

As a Graphic Designer, I often work with large format printing and need advice on the best export settings for PDF files to ensure sharp, high-resolution output. Can ChatGPT help me understand the ideal settings for large format print production?

Idea: Print file preflight tools

Recommendations for preflight tools that can help ensure print files are error-free and ready for printing.

Example Prompt 1:
Hey ChatGPT, as a graphic designer, I'm looking for recommendations on print file preflight tools that can help me ensure my designs are error-free and ready for printing. Can you suggest some reliable preflight tools for print files?

Example Prompt 2:
ChatGPT, I need your help as a graphic designer to find print file preflight tools that can assist me in ensuring my print files are error-free and ready for printing. Can you provide me with a list of recommended preflight tools for this purpose?

Example Prompt 3:
As a graphic designer, I'm in need of print file preflight tools to help me ensure my designs are error-free and ready for printing. Can you assist me by recommending some reliable preflight tools specifically tailored for print files?

Example Prompt 4:
ChatGPT, I'm seeking your expertise as a graphic designer to help me find print file preflight tools that can ensure my print files are error-free and ready for printing. Can you provide me with a comprehensive list of preflight tools that are suitable for this purpose?

Idea: Print file mockup resources

Resources for creating realistic mockups of print materials to present to clients or for portfolio purposes.

Example Prompt 1:
Hey ChatGPT, I need your help in finding high-quality print

file mockup resources for creating realistic mockups of brochures, business cards, and other print materials. Can you suggest some websites or tools that offer a wide range of mockup templates for different print materials?

Example Prompt 2:
ChatGPT, I'm looking for resources to help me create professional-looking mockups of print materials such as flyers, posters, and packaging. Can you recommend any online platforms or software that provide customizable mockup templates and easy-to-use tools for editing and customizing print files?

Example Prompt 3:
I'm in need of print file mockup resources to enhance my portfolio and impress potential clients. ChatGPT, can you assist me in finding websites or design communities where I can access a variety of print mockup templates and resources to showcase my design work in a realistic and professional manner?

Example Prompt 4:
ChatGPT, I'm a graphic designer seeking print file mockup resources to elevate my presentation of print materials to clients. Do you have any recommendations for online marketplaces or design tools that offer a diverse collection of print mockup templates and resources to help me create visually appealing and realistic mockups for my design projects?

Idea: Print file delivery methods

Best practices for delivering print files to printers, including file transfer methods and specifications.

Example Prompt 1:
As a Graphic Designer, I need guidance on the best file delivery methods for print files. Can you provide a comprehensive overview of the different file transfer methods and specifications that are commonly used in the industry?

Example Prompt 2:

I'm looking for advice on how to effectively deliver print files to printers. Can you share best practices for ensuring that the files are transferred securely and accurately, including any specific file format requirements or other technical specifications?

Example Prompt 3:

As a professional in the graphic design field, I often need to send print files to printers. Can you provide a step-by-step guide on the most efficient and reliable methods for delivering these files, taking into account factors such as file size, resolution, and color management?

Example Prompt 4:

I'm seeking expert advice on the most reliable and efficient ways to transfer print files to printers. Can you offer insights into the latest file delivery methods and specifications that are recommended for ensuring high-quality print output?

USER INTERFACE
DESIGN BASICS

USER-CENTRIC CREATION: BASICS OF UI DESIGN

In today's fast-paced digital landscape, the synergy between graphic designers and artificial intelligence is paramount for creating exceptional user interfaces. In this chapter, we'll delve into the core principles of UI design that will help you craft intuitive and visually appealing digital experiences. To illustrate these principles, let's follow Sarah, a talented graphic designer, as she navigates her role in a world powered by AI.

Clarity is Key:

Sarah understands that clarity is the cornerstone of effective UI design. When working on a mobile app, she ensures that every element, from buttons to icons, conveys its purpose. AI-powered tools like ChatGPT assist her by generating concise and user-friendly microcopy. Clear instructions and error messages make the user's journey seamless.

Simplicity is Genius:

Sarah embraces the mantra 'less is more.' She uses AI-generated design recommendations to streamline complex interfaces. ChatGPT suggests minimalist color palettes, typography choices, and layout options. This allows her to create interfaces that are both elegant and user-friendly, a balance AI can help her achieve effortlessly.

Consistency Matters:

As Sarah designs various screens for her app, consistency remains at the forefront of her mind. She employs AI to generate style guides, ensuring that elements like button sizes and font choices are uniform across the interface. This consistency enhances the user's experience by reducing cognitive load.

Human-Centered Design:

Sarah recognizes the importance of empathizing with the end user. AI tools, like sentiment analysis powered by ChatGPT, help her understand user feedback and adapt the design accordingly. By incorporating user perspectives into her work, she ensures that the final product aligns with their needs and preferences.

User Flow Optimization:

AI-driven analytics tools assist Sarah in tracking user interactions within the app. By analyzing this data, she identifies pain points and bottlenecks in the user journey. With ChatGPT's insights, she can make informed decisions to optimize the user flow, leading to a more satisfying experience.

Adaptation and Personalization:

In a world where personalization reigns supreme, AI lends Sarah a helping hand. ChatGPT suggests ways to incorporate dynamic content and adaptive layouts. By tailoring the UI to each user's preferences and behavior, she creates interfaces that feel tailor-made.

Testing and Iteration:

Sarah knows that UI design is an ongoing process. AI-driven A/B testing helps her compare different design variations quickly. ChatGPT provides insights on which elements resonate with users, enabling her to iterate and refine the interface continuously.

As Sarah skillfully integrates AI-powered tools like ChatGPT into her design process, she finds herself not just as a designer but as a creator of harmonious digital experiences. With a focus on clarity, simplicity, consistency, empathy, optimization, personalization, and ongoing improvement, Sarah's UI designs reflect the perfect fusion of art and AI-driven science.

In conclusion, graphic designers like Sarah have the opportunity to leverage AI to enhance their craft and create user interfaces that captivate and delight. By embracing the principles outlined in this chapter, they can stay at the forefront of the ever-evolving field of UI design, ensuring their work stands out in the digital landscape.

Task: Color theory

Help with understanding and choosing appropriate color schemes for user interfaces

Example Prompt 1:

Can you explain the basics of color theory and how it applies to user interface design?

Example Prompt 2:
What are some common color schemes used in user interface design, and when is it appropriate to use each one?

Example Prompt 3:
How can I use color to create hierarchy and emphasis in my user interface designs?

Example Prompt 4:
Can you provide examples of user interfaces that effectively use color to enhance the user experience?

Task: Typography

Assistance with selecting and pairing fonts for better readability and visual appeal

Example Prompt 1:
Can you suggest a font pairing that would work well for a modern and clean website design? I'm looking for something that is easy to read but also visually appealing.

Example Prompt 2:
I'm working on a poster design and I'm struggling to find the right combination of fonts. Can you recommend a headline font that pairs well with a more subtle and elegant body font?

Example Prompt 3:
I'm designing a magazine layout and I want to make sure the typography is cohesive throughout. Can you help me choose a font combination that will work well for both headlines and body text?

Example Prompt 4:
I'm creating a presentation and I want to make sure the fonts I use are professional and easy to read. Can you provide some guidance on selecting fonts that will enhance the visual appeal of my slides?

Task: Layout design

Suggestions for creating balanced and visually appealing layouts for user interfaces

Example Prompt 1:

How can I effectively use white space to create a clean and balanced layout for a user interface?

Example Prompt 2:

What are some techniques for creating visual hierarchy in a user interface design to guide the user's attention?

Example Prompt 3:

Can you provide examples of successful user interface layouts that effectively balance text and imagery?

Example Prompt 4:

What are some best practices for creating a grid-based layout for a user interface design to ensure visual harmony and organization?

Task: Iconography

Assistance with creating or choosing appropriate icons for user interfaces

Example Prompt 1:

Can you suggest some iconography that would effectively communicate 'settings' or 'preferences' in a user interface?

Example Prompt 2:

I'm looking for icons that represent different file types (e.g. document, image, video). Any recommendations?

Example Prompt 3:

What are some commonly used icons for navigation (e.g. home, back, forward) that are easily recognizable and intuitive for users?

Example Prompt 4:

I need help choosing icons for a messaging app - what are some universally understood symbols for 'send', 'receive', and 'delete'?

Task: User experience (UX) principles

Guidance on incorporating UX best practices into user interface design

Example Prompt 1:
How can I ensure that my user interface design prioritizes ease of use and intuitive navigation for the best user experience?

Example Prompt 2:
What are some effective ways to incorporate user feedback into the design process to improve the overall user experience?

Example Prompt 3:
Can you provide examples of successful user interface designs that effectively utilize UX principles to enhance user satisfaction and engagement?

Example Prompt 4:
What are some key considerations for designing a user interface that is accessible and inclusive for all users, regardless of their abilities or limitations?

Task: Accessibility

Tips for designing user interfaces that are accessible to all users, including those with disabilities

Example Prompt 1:
How can we ensure that our user interface designs are accessible to all users, including those with visual impairments or color blindness?

Example Prompt 2:
What are some best practices for designing user interfaces that are easily navigable for users with motor disabilities or limited dexterity?

Example Prompt 3:

Can you provide tips for creating accessible user interfaces that are compatible with screen readers and other assistive technologies?

Example Prompt 4:
What are some common pitfalls to avoid when designing user interfaces to ensure accessibility for users with disabilities?

Task: Responsive design

Help with designing user interfaces that work well on various devices and screen sizes

Example Prompt 1:
How can I ensure that my user interface design is responsive and works well on different devices and screen sizes?

Example Prompt 2:
What are some best practices for creating a responsive design that adapts to various screen sizes and resolutions?

Example Prompt 3:
Can you provide examples of successful user interfaces that effectively utilize responsive design principles?

Example Prompt 4:
What tools or resources do you recommend for testing and optimizing the responsiveness of a user interface design?

Task: Prototyping

Assistance with creating interactive prototypes to test and refine user interface designs

Example Prompt 1:
Can you help me create a prototype for a new mobile app interface design? I want to test out different user interactions and refine the overall user experience.

Example Prompt 2:
I'm looking for assistance in prototyping a website interface with

interactive elements. Can you guide me through the process and provide tips for refining the design?

Example Prompt 3:
I need help creating a prototype for a new digital product. How can I use interactive prototypes to gather feedback and improve the user interface design?

Example Prompt 4:
I'm interested in prototyping a new interactive feature for an existing product. Can you assist me in creating a prototype to test and refine the user interface design?

Task: User testing

Guidance on conducting user testing to gather feedback and improve user interface designs

Example Prompt 1:
How can I effectively gather user feedback on my interface designs to ensure they are intuitive and user-friendly?

Example Prompt 2:
What are some best practices for conducting user testing to gather valuable insights for improving my interface designs?

Example Prompt 3:
Can you provide guidance on creating user testing scenarios that accurately reflect real-world usage of my interface designs?

Example Prompt 4:
What are some methods for analyzing and interpreting user feedback from testing to make informed decisions for improving my interface designs?

Task: Design tools

Recommendations for tools and software to use for user interface design.

Example Prompt 1:
What are some essential design tools and software for creating user interfaces? Any recommendations for beginners?

Example Prompt 2:
Can you suggest some user-friendly design tools and software that are suitable for creating interactive prototypes and wireframes?

Example Prompt 3:
I'm looking for design tools and software that offer a good balance of functionality and ease of use for creating visually appealing user interfaces. Any suggestions?

Example Prompt 4:
As a graphic designer, what are your go-to design tools and software for creating seamless user experiences? Any recommendations for collaborative design platforms?

Idea: Interactive UI design tutorials

ChatGPT can provide step-by-step tutorials on creating interactive user interfaces, including best practices and design principles.

Example Prompt 1:
Hey ChatGPT, can you provide a step-by-step tutorial on creating interactive user interfaces, focusing on best practices and design principles? I'd love to learn more about UI design from a graphic designer's perspective.

Example Prompt 2:
ChatGPT, I'm looking to improve my skills in creating interactive user interfaces. Can you guide me through a tutorial that covers the essential design principles and best practices for UI design?

Example Prompt 3:
As a graphic designer, I'm interested in learning more about creating interactive user interfaces. Can ChatGPT provide a

tutorial that breaks down the process and offers insights into effective UI design?

Example Prompt 4:

I'm seeking guidance on creating interactive user interfaces as a graphic designer. Can ChatGPT offer a tutorial that delves into the step-by-step process and highlights key design principles for UI design?

Idea: UI design critique sessions

ChatGPT can provide feedback on UI designs, pointing out areas for improvement and suggesting alternative approaches.

Example Prompt 1:

Hey ChatGPT, I'm working on a new UI design for a mobile app and I'd love your feedback. Can you provide a critique of the overall layout, color scheme, and user flow, and suggest any alternative approaches that might improve the design?

Example Prompt 2:

ChatGPT, I'm in the process of redesigning a website and I'd like your input on the UI. Can you review the navigation, typography, and visual hierarchy, and offer suggestions for enhancing the user experience?

Example Prompt 3:

I'm creating a new dashboard interface for a data analytics tool and I'd appreciate your perspective, ChatGPT. Could you analyze the data visualization, layout, and interaction design, and propose any improvements or alternative design solutions?

Example Prompt 4:

ChatGPT, I'm working on a UI design for a new e-commerce platform and I'd like to get your insights. Can you evaluate the product display, checkout process, and overall usability, and provide recommendations for optimizing the user interface?

Idea: UI design tool recommendations

ChatGPT can recommend the best tools and software for UI design based on specific needs and preferences.

Example Prompt 1:

Hey ChatGPT, I'm looking for a UI design tool that is user-friendly and has a wide range of templates. Can you recommend the best software for me?

Example Prompt 2:

I need a UI design tool that allows for easy collaboration and sharing of designs with my team. Can you suggest a tool that fits this requirement?

Example Prompt 3:

I'm in search of a UI design tool that offers advanced prototyping features and seamless integration with other design software. What would you recommend for this?

Example Prompt 4:

I'm looking for a UI design tool that has a strong focus on mobile app design and offers a variety of mobile-specific features. Can you suggest a tool that excels in this area?

Idea: UI design trend analysis

ChatGPT can analyze current UI design trends and provide insights on how to incorporate them into designs.

Example Prompt 1:

Hey ChatGPT, I'm looking to stay ahead of the curve with my UI designs. Can you analyze current UI design trends and provide insights on how to incorporate them into my projects?

Example Prompt 2:

As a graphic designer, I'm always looking for new inspiration for my UI designs. Can you help me by analyzing the latest UI design trends and offering suggestions for incorporating them into my work?

Example Prompt 3:
I want to ensure that my UI designs are modern and up-to-date. Can you provide an analysis of current UI design trends and offer recommendations for how I can integrate them into my designs?

Example Prompt 4:
I'm interested in learning more about the latest UI design trends and how I can apply them to my projects. Can you provide insights and analysis on current UI design trends to help me stay on top of the latest developments?

Idea: UI design color theory

ChatGPT can explain the principles of color theory and how to apply them effectively in UI design.

Example Prompt 1:
Can you provide an overview of the principles of color theory and how they can be applied to create visually appealing UI designs?

Example Prompt 2:
Please explain the psychological effects of different colors and how they can be used to evoke specific emotions in UI design.

Example Prompt 3:
How can contrasting and complementary colors be used effectively in UI design to create a visually balanced and harmonious user experience?

Example Prompt 4:
Can you provide examples of successful UI designs that effectively utilize color theory principles, and explain how these choices contribute to the overall user experience?

Idea: UI design typography tips

ChatGPT can provide tips on choosing and using typography effectively in UI design.

Example Prompt 1:
Hey ChatGPT, can you provide some tips on choosing the right typography for UI design? I'm looking for advice on how to make my text stand out and be easily readable on my website.

Example Prompt 2:
I'm working on a new app and I want to make sure the typography is on point for the UI design. Can you give me some guidance on how to choose the best fonts and styles to create a modern and user-friendly interface?

Example Prompt 3:
I'm struggling with typography choices for my website's UI design. Can you help me understand how to effectively use different font weights, sizes, and styles to create a cohesive and visually appealing design?

Example Prompt 4:
I'm a graphic designer working on a new project and I need some advice on typography for the UI design. Can you provide some tips on creating a typographic hierarchy and ensuring readability for different screen sizes and resolutions?

Idea: UI design accessibility guidelines

ChatGPT can provide guidelines and best practices for creating accessible user interfaces for all users.

Example Prompt 1:
Hey ChatGPT, can you provide a comprehensive list of UI design accessibility guidelines and best practices for creating inclusive user interfaces?

Example Prompt 2:
I need some assistance in understanding how to make my user interface more accessible for all users. Can you provide me with

some tips and recommendations for designing an inclusive UI?

Example Prompt 3:
As a graphic designer, I want to ensure that my UI designs are accessible to all users. Can you help me by providing some guidelines and best practices for creating inclusive user interfaces?

Example Prompt 4:
I'm looking for support in making my UI designs more accessible. Can you provide me with some insights and recommendations for designing user interfaces that are inclusive for all users?

Idea: UI design prototyping techniques

ChatGPT can suggest prototyping techniques and tools for creating interactive UI prototypes.

Example Prompt 1:
Hey ChatGPT, I'm looking for some innovative prototyping techniques for UI design. Can you suggest some tools and methods for creating interactive UI prototypes that will impress my clients?

Example Prompt 2:
As a graphic designer, I'm always on the lookout for new ways to prototype UI designs. Can ChatGPT recommend some cutting-edge techniques and tools for creating interactive and visually stunning UI prototypes?

Example Prompt 3:
I'm in need of some fresh ideas for prototyping UI designs. ChatGPT, can you provide me with some advanced prototyping techniques and tools that will help me bring my UI designs to life?

Example Prompt 4:
ChatGPT, as a graphic designer, I'm interested in exploring new prototyping techniques for UI design. Can you suggest some modern and efficient tools and methods for creating interactive UI prototypes that will elevate my design work?

Idea: UI design layout principles

ChatGPT can explain the principles of effective layout design for user interfaces.

Example Prompt 1:
Can you provide an overview of the key principles of effective UI design layout, including balance, hierarchy, and alignment?

Example Prompt 2:
Please explain how to create a visually appealing and user-friendly UI design layout, considering factors such as proximity, contrast, and repetition.

Example Prompt 3:
I'd like to understand how to use grid systems and spacing to create a cohesive and organized UI design layout. Can you provide some insights on this?

Example Prompt 4:
Could you share some best practices for incorporating typography and color theory into UI design layout to enhance user experience and visual appeal?

Idea: UI design usability testing methods

ChatGPT can suggest methods for conducting usability testing on UI designs and interpreting the results.

Example Prompt 1:
Hey ChatGPT, as a graphic designer, I'm looking for methods to conduct usability testing on UI designs. Can you suggest some effective techniques and tools for gathering user feedback on the usability of my designs?

Example Prompt 2:
ChatGPT, I need help interpreting the results of my UI design usability testing. Can you provide insights on how to analyze user

feedback and make improvements based on the findings?

Example Prompt 3:
As a graphic designer, I want to ensure that my UI designs are user-friendly. Can ChatGPT recommend best practices for conducting usability testing and incorporating user feedback into the design process?

Example Prompt 4:
ChatGPT, I'm interested in learning about different approaches to usability testing for UI designs. Can you provide guidance on how to choose the right methods for testing and evaluating the usability of my designs?

Idea: UI design responsive design principles

ChatGPT can explain the principles of responsive design and how to create UIs that work across different devices and screen sizes.

Example Prompt 1:
Can you provide a comprehensive explanation of the key principles of responsive design for UIs? How can designers ensure that their UIs are adaptable and functional across various devices and screen sizes?

Example Prompt 2:
Please outline the best practices for creating responsive UI designs that prioritize user experience and accessibility. What are the main considerations when designing for different screen resolutions and orientations?

Example Prompt 3:
I'd like to understand the role of fluid grids, flexible images, and media queries in achieving responsive UI design. Can you provide a detailed breakdown of how these elements contribute to a seamless user interface experience?

Example Prompt 4:

Could you walk me through the process of implementing responsive design principles in UI creation? What are the common challenges and how can designers overcome them to deliver a consistent and user-friendly interface?

Idea: UI design user experience (UX) principles

ChatGPT can provide insights into UX principles and how they relate to UI design, helping designers create more user-friendly interfaces.

Example Prompt 1:
Can you provide insights into the key UX principles that should be considered when designing a user interface? How do these principles contribute to creating a more user-friendly experience for the end user?

Example Prompt 2:
I'm looking to understand how ChatGPT can help me incorporate UX principles into my UI design process. Can you provide examples or case studies where ChatGPT has supported designers in creating more intuitive and user-friendly interfaces?

Example Prompt 3:
I'm interested in learning more about the relationship between UX principles and UI design. Can ChatGPT provide guidance on how to prioritize and implement these principles to enhance the overall user experience?

Example Prompt 4:
As a graphic designer, I want to ensure that my UI designs are aligned with best practices in UX principles. How can ChatGPT assist me in identifying and incorporating these principles into my design process?

PORTFOLIO DEVELOPMENT

SHOWCASE OF SKILLS: ASSEMBLING A POWERFUL PORTFOLIO

In the competitive world of graphic design, a standout portfolio is your ticket to success. As we delve into the realm of portfolio development, let's follow the journey of Mark, a seasoned graphic designer, and explore how artificial intelligence, with the assistance of ChatGPT, can help him create a compelling showcase of his skills and versatility.

Curation is Key:

Mark understands that a cluttered portfolio can overwhelm potential clients or employers. AI-driven content analysis tools, powered by ChatGPT, assist him in selecting the most impactful pieces. By focusing on his best work, Mark ensures his portfolio reflects his true talents.

Personal Branding:

Mark recognizes the importance of a consistent visual identity. With ChatGPT's guidance, he crafts a unique brand image, incorporating AI-suggested color palettes and typography choices. This not only enhances his portfolio's aesthetic appeal but also communicates his design sensibilities.

Storytelling Through Projects:

Rather than merely showcasing images, Mark uses AI-generated copy to tell the story behind each project. ChatGPT helps him craft compelling narratives, describing the problem-solving process, design choices, and outcomes. This narrative adds depth and context to his work.

Diverse Range of Work:

Mark knows that a well-rounded portfolio is essential. AI-driven trend analysis tools assist him in identifying emerging design styles and techniques. By integrating these insights, he ensures his portfolio demonstrates his adaptability and relevance in a rapidly evolving industry.

Interactive Elements:

With AI's assistance, Mark adds interactive elements to his digital portfolio. ChatGPT helps him create engaging microinteractions and animations that showcase his design skills in action. These dynamic features capture the viewer's attention and provide a memorable experience.

AI-Powered Search Functionality:

Mark incorporates an AI-powered search feature into his portfolio website, allowing visitors to find specific projects quickly. ChatGPT's natural language processing capabilities enable users to search by keywords, making it easier to navigate his extensive body of work.

User Feedback and Iteration:

After launching his AI-enhanced portfolio, Mark uses sentiment analysis powered by ChatGPT to gather user feedback. This data helps him identify areas for improvement and refine his portfolio over time, ensuring it continues to resonate with his target audience.

As Mark harnesses the capabilities of artificial intelligence, his portfolio evolves into a compelling showcase of his design prowess. With a focus on curation, personal branding, storytelling, diversity, interactivity, and continuous improvement, Mark's portfolio not only highlights his skills but also engages and captivates his audience.

In conclusion, for graphic designers like Mark, the integration of AI tools like ChatGPT can be a game-changer in portfolio development. By following the principles outlined in this chapter, designers can create portfolios that not only reflect their abilities but also leave a lasting impression on potential clients and employers in the ever-competitive world of graphic design.

Task: Researching design trends

ChatGPT can provide insights and updates on current design trends and popular styles.

Example Prompt 1:
Can you provide me with insights on the latest color palettes and combinations that are trending in graphic design?

Example Prompt 2:
What are some popular typography styles and fonts that are currently being used in design?

Example Prompt 3:

I'm interested in learning about the emerging trends in web design, particularly in terms of layout and user interface. Can you share any recent developments in this area?

Example Prompt 4:
I'd like to stay updated on the latest design trends in branding and logo design. Can you provide me with information on what's currently popular and effective in this space?

Task: Brainstorming project ideas

ChatGPT can help generate creative ideas for portfolio projects based on your interests and skills.

Example Prompt 1:
I'm a graphic designer looking to create a new portfolio project that showcases my skills in branding and logo design. Can you help me brainstorm some unique business concepts that I can create branding materials for?

Example Prompt 2:
I want to expand my portfolio with some digital illustration projects. Can you suggest some interesting themes or subjects that I can explore in my illustrations?

Example Prompt 3:
I'm interested in creating a series of social media graphics for a specific niche market. Can you help me brainstorm some ideas for content and design styles that would resonate with this audience?

Example Prompt 4:
I'm looking to add some web design projects to my portfolio. Can you help me come up with some innovative website concepts that I can use to showcase my skills in user interface and user experience design?

Task: Creating project outlines

ChatGPT can assist in outlining the key details and objectives for each portfolio project.

Example Prompt 1:
Can you help me brainstorm and outline the key design elements and objectives for a new branding project for a tech startup?

Example Prompt 2:
I need assistance in outlining the key details and objectives for a website redesign project for a fashion e-commerce brand. Can you provide some guidance?

Example Prompt 3:
I'm looking to create a project outline for a social media campaign design project for a non-profit organization. Can you help me identify the key goals and design elements?

Example Prompt 4:
I'm working on a packaging design project for a new line of beauty products. Can you assist me in outlining the key details and objectives for this project?

Task: Writing project descriptions

ChatGPT can help craft compelling and informative descriptions for each project in your portfolio.

Example Prompt 1:
Create a project description for a branding and logo design project, highlighting the client's goals and the creative process behind the final design.

Example Prompt 2:
Craft a project description for a website redesign project, emphasizing the user experience improvements and visual enhancements implemented.

Example Prompt 3:
Write a project description for a social media campaign design, showcasing the strategic approach and the impact on audience

engagement and brand awareness.

Example Prompt 4:
Develop a project description for a print design project, focusing on the unique concept, visual elements, and the intended message conveyed through the design.

Task: Generating design concepts

ChatGPT can provide inspiration and generate initial design concepts for your portfolio pieces.

Example Prompt 1:
Can you suggest some modern and minimalist design concepts for a tech startup's branding?

Example Prompt 2:
I'm looking for some fresh ideas for a nature-inspired logo design. Can you help me brainstorm some concepts?

Example Prompt 3:
I need some creative concepts for a food packaging design. Can you provide some initial ideas to get me started?

Example Prompt 4:
I'm working on a website redesign for a fashion brand. Can you help me generate some innovative design concepts to explore?

Task: Reviewing and refining portfolio pieces

ChatGPT can offer feedback and suggestions for improving the visual appeal and effectiveness of your portfolio pieces.

Example Prompt 1:
Can you provide a brief description of the goal or message you aimed to convey with this portfolio piece? ChatGPT can offer suggestions on how to enhance the visual elements to better align with your intended message.

Example Prompt 2:

Please share the target audience for this portfolio piece. ChatGPT can provide feedback on how to tailor the design to better resonate with your intended viewers.

Example Prompt 3:
What specific aspects of this portfolio piece are you looking to improve? ChatGPT can offer recommendations on refining the layout, color scheme, typography, or any other visual elements.

Example Prompt 4:
Are there any specific design principles or techniques you'd like feedback on for this portfolio piece? ChatGPT can provide insights on how to enhance the overall visual appeal and effectiveness based on design best practices.

Task: Organizing and categorizing portfolio content

ChatGPT can assist in structuring and categorizing your portfolio content for easy navigation and presentation.

Example Prompt 1:
Can you help me create a visually appealing layout for my portfolio that effectively organizes my work into different categories such as branding, web design, and print materials?

Example Prompt 2:
I need assistance in creating a system for tagging and categorizing my portfolio pieces based on industry, client type, and project type. Can you help me with this?

Example Prompt 3:
I'm looking for a way to organize my portfolio content in a way that showcases my skills and expertise in different design disciplines such as illustration, typography, and photography. Can you provide guidance on how to achieve this?

Example Prompt 4:

I want to create a portfolio that is easy to navigate and allows viewers to filter and sort through my work based on criteria such as date, project type, and client. How can I achieve this with ChatGPT's assistance?

Idea: Online portfolio website

ChatGPT can help with content writing for the website, including artist statements, project descriptions, and bio.

Example Prompt 1:
Create a compelling artist statement for my online portfolio website that captures my creative vision and artistic journey.

Example Prompt 2:
Craft engaging project descriptions for each of my featured works on my online portfolio website, highlighting the inspiration and process behind each piece.

Example Prompt 3:
Develop a captivating bio for my online portfolio website that showcases my background, artistic influences, and accomplishments in a professional yet engaging manner.

Example Prompt 4:
Assist in writing compelling content for the 'About' section of my online portfolio website, conveying my passion for art and design in a way that resonates with visitors.

Idea: Portfolio review and critique service

ChatGPT can provide feedback on design choices, layout, and overall presentation of the portfolio.

Example Prompt 1:
Hey ChatGPT, as a graphic designer, I'd love your help in reviewing and critiquing my portfolio. Can you provide feedback on the design choices, layout, and overall presentation of my work?

Example Prompt 2:
ChatGPT, I'm looking for a portfolio review and critique service for my graphic design work. Can you help me by providing detailed feedback on my design choices, layout, and overall presentation?

Example Prompt 3:
As a graphic designer, I'm seeking a professional critique of my portfolio. Can ChatGPT assist me by offering feedback on my design choices, layout, and overall presentation to help me improve?

Example Prompt 4:
I'm in need of a portfolio review and critique for my graphic design portfolio. ChatGPT, can you provide detailed feedback on my design choices, layout, and overall presentation to help me refine my work?

Idea: Customized portfolio templates

ChatGPT can assist in creating unique and visually appealing portfolio templates for different design styles.

Example Prompt 1:
Create a modern and minimalist portfolio template that showcases clean lines and bold typography. Consider using a monochromatic color scheme to enhance the overall aesthetic.

Example Prompt 2:
Design a portfolio template with a focus on showcasing photography and visual artwork. Incorporate dynamic layouts and interactive elements to engage the viewer and highlight the creative work.

Example Prompt 3:
Develop a portfolio template with a vintage-inspired design, featuring ornate borders, decorative elements, and a muted color palette. Emphasize a sense of nostalgia and timeless elegance in the overall presentation.

Example Prompt 4:
Craft a portfolio template that reflects a futuristic and tech-inspired aesthetic, utilizing sleek and metallic elements, geometric shapes, and vibrant, high-contrast colors. Consider incorporating interactive features to create an immersive viewing experience.

Idea: Social media promotion strategy

ChatGPT can help in developing a social media content calendar and writing engaging captions for portfolio posts.

Example Prompt 1:
Create a social media promotion strategy for a graphic design portfolio, including a content calendar and engaging caption ideas for each post.

Example Prompt 2:
Develop a monthly content calendar for social media promotion of a graphic design portfolio, with engaging caption suggestions for each post.

Example Prompt 3:
Assist in crafting a social media promotion plan for a graphic design portfolio, including a content calendar and captivating captions for portfolio posts.

Example Prompt 4:
Help in strategizing a social media promotion approach for a graphic design portfolio, providing a content calendar and writing compelling captions for each post.

Idea: Client case studies

ChatGPT can assist in writing detailed case studies for projects in the portfolio, highlighting the design process and outcomes.

Example Prompt 1:
Prompt: "Create a detailed case study for our recent branding

project, showcasing the design process from concept to final product. Include client feedback and the impact of the new branding on their business."

Example Prompt 2:
Prompt: "Assist in writing a comprehensive case study for our website redesign project, emphasizing the user experience improvements and the design choices made to enhance functionality and aesthetics."

Example Prompt 3:
Prompt: "Help us craft a case study for our packaging design project, focusing on the creative process, material selection, and the positive impact on sales and customer perception."

Example Prompt 4:
Prompt: "Support in developing a case study for our print campaign, highlighting the design strategy, target audience engagement, and the measurable results achieved through the visual elements and messaging."

Idea: Portfolio presentation materials

ChatGPT can help in creating presentation materials such as pitch decks, slideshows, and PDF portfolios.

Example Prompt 1:
Create a visually stunning pitch deck for my upcoming business presentation, incorporating our brand colors and logo. Include compelling graphics and concise text to effectively communicate our key points.

Example Prompt 2:
Design a professional slideshow for my portfolio presentation, showcasing my work in a visually appealing and organized manner. Use creative layouts and typography to enhance the overall aesthetic.

Example Prompt 3:

Assist me in creating a PDF portfolio that effectively highlights my skills and previous projects. Incorporate interactive elements and visually engaging graphics to captivate potential clients or employers.

Example Prompt 4:
Help me develop a visually impactful presentation material for my upcoming conference, incorporating infographics, charts, and other visual aids to effectively convey complex information in a clear and engaging manner.

Idea: Personal branding strategy

ChatGPT can assist in developing a personal branding strategy, including logo design, color palette selection, and brand messaging.

Example Prompt 1:
Hey ChatGPT, I'm looking to develop a personal branding strategy for my freelance business. Can you help me brainstorm logo design ideas and suggest a color palette that reflects my brand's personality and values?

Example Prompt 2:
I'm in the process of rebranding my personal blog and I could use some assistance with brand messaging. Can you help me craft a compelling brand story and key messaging points that resonate with my audience?

Example Prompt 3:
As a graphic designer, I'm looking to revamp my personal brand. Can you assist me in creating a unique and memorable logo that represents my design style and aesthetic?

Example Prompt 4:
I'm a new entrepreneur and I need help establishing a cohesive personal brand. Can you guide me through the process of selecting a color palette that aligns with my brand's identity and values?

Idea: Networking and outreach emails

ChatGPT can help in crafting personalized outreach emails to potential clients or collaborators to showcase the portfolio.

Example Prompt 1:

Create a personalized outreach email template for networking and collaboration opportunities, incorporating our portfolio and highlighting our unique design style.

Example Prompt 2:

Assist in drafting a compelling introductory email to potential clients, emphasizing our design expertise and previous successful projects.

Example Prompt 3:

Help in customizing outreach emails to different target audiences, showcasing relevant design work and tailoring the message to their specific needs and interests.

Example Prompt 4:

Support in creating visually appealing email graphics and attachments to accompany our outreach emails, effectively showcasing our design portfolio and capabilities.

Idea: Portfolio print materials

ChatGPT can assist in creating print materials such as business cards, postcards, and leave-behinds for in-person portfolio presentations.

Example Prompt 1:

Hey ChatGPT, I'm a graphic designer looking to create print materials for my portfolio presentations. Can you help me design a unique and eye-catching business card that reflects my style and expertise?

Example Prompt 2:

ChatGPT, I need assistance in designing postcards that showcase my best work and leave a lasting impression on potential clients during in-person portfolio presentations. Can you help me create a design that stands out?

Example Prompt 3:
I'm in need of leave-behinds to accompany my portfolio presentations, ChatGPT. Can you help me come up with creative and professional print materials that effectively showcase my design work and leave a lasting impact on potential clients?

Example Prompt 4:
ChatGPT, as a graphic designer, I want to create print materials that reflect my creativity and expertise. Can you assist me in designing business cards, postcards, and leave-behinds that effectively represent my design style and leave a memorable impression on viewers?

Idea: Portfolio video walkthroughs

ChatGPT can help in scripting and creating video walkthroughs of the portfolio, providing a dynamic way to showcase work.

Example Prompt 1:
Create a script for a video walkthrough of my graphic design portfolio, highlighting key projects and explaining the creative process behind each one.

Example Prompt 2:
Assist in developing a storyboard for a visually engaging video walkthrough of my portfolio, incorporating dynamic transitions and visual effects to showcase my work.

Example Prompt 3:
Help me write a compelling voiceover script for a video walkthrough of my portfolio, capturing the essence of each project and conveying my passion for graphic design.

Example Prompt 4:
Collaborate with me to create a polished and professional video walkthrough of my portfolio, utilizing ChatGPT's expertise to craft a visually stunning and informative showcase of my design work.

Idea: Portfolio curation and organization

ChatGPT can assist in organizing and curating the portfolio content, ensuring a cohesive and impactful presentation.

Example Prompt 1:
ChatGPT, can you help me create a visually appealing layout for my portfolio, ensuring that all the content is organized in a cohesive and impactful manner?

Example Prompt 2:
I need assistance in selecting the best images and designs for my portfolio. Can you help me curate the content to create a strong visual impact?

Example Prompt 3:
ChatGPT, I'm looking to organize my portfolio in a way that highlights my skills and experience. Can you assist me in structuring the content for maximum impact?

Example Prompt 4:
I want to ensure that my portfolio has a consistent visual theme throughout. Can you help me organize and curate the content to achieve a cohesive and impactful presentation?

Idea: Portfolio website SEO optimization

ChatGPT can help in optimizing the portfolio website for search engines by providing relevant keywords and meta descriptions.

Example Prompt 1:
Hey ChatGPT, I'm a graphic designer looking to optimize my

portfolio website for search engines. Can you help me come up with relevant keywords and meta descriptions to improve my website's SEO?

Example Prompt 2:

As a graphic designer, I want to make sure my portfolio website is easily discoverable on search engines. Can you assist me in identifying the best keywords and crafting effective meta descriptions for my website?

Example Prompt 3:

I'm in need of some SEO optimization for my portfolio website as a graphic designer. Can you provide me with suggestions for relevant keywords and help me create compelling meta descriptions to improve my website's search engine visibility?

Example Prompt 4:

I'm looking to enhance the SEO of my portfolio website as a graphic designer. Can you guide me in identifying the most effective keywords and assist me in writing impactful meta descriptions to boost my website's search engine rankings?

TREND ANALYSIS
AND ADAPTATION

TRENDSPOTTING: STAYING AHEAD IN DESIGN

In the ever-evolving landscape of graphic design, staying attuned to current trends is essential for maintaining relevance and creativity. Let's follow the journey of Lisa, a talented graphic designer, as she harnesses the power of artificial intelligence, specifically ChatGPT, to analyze design trends and infuse them into her projects creatively.

Trendspotting with AI:

Lisa begins her journey by using AI-powered trend analysis tools, fueled by ChatGPT's data-crunching capabilities. By scouring design forums, social media, and industry publications, she identifies emerging trends in typography, color schemes, and design styles.

Adaptation is the Key:

Rather than blindly following trends, Lisa leverages AI to understand the underlying principles that make certain design trends popular. She deconstructs these trends to find creative ways to adapt them to her projects while preserving her unique style.

Embrace Fusion:

Lisa understands that combining different trends can lead to innovative and eye-catching designs. With ChatGPT's assistance, she experiments with hybrid designs, merging elements from various trends to create something entirely fresh and unexpected.

Test the Waters:

Before implementing trend-inspired changes in her client projects, Lisa uses AI-generated A/B testing to gauge audience reactions. This data-driven approach helps her fine-tune her adaptations for maximum impact.

Personalization and Branding:

Lisa knows that blindly following trends can dilute her brand identity. She uses AI to tailor trends to align with her clients' brands. ChatGPT assists in creating personalized adaptations that reflect the essence of each brand while incorporating the latest design trends.

Stay Updated:

With AI's help, Lisa sets up real-time trend alerts. ChatGPT continuously monitors design trends, allowing her to adapt her projects as trends evolve, ensuring her work remains fresh and relevant.

Ethical Considerations:

Lisa remains mindful of the ethical aspects of design trends. She uses AI-driven sentiment analysis to gauge public opinion on emerging trends and ensures her adaptations align with her clients' values and the expectations of their target audience.

By embracing the symbiotic relationship between artificial intelligence and graphic design, Lisa breathes new life into her projects. She combines her creative instincts with AI's trend analysis capabilities to produce work that's both current and uniquely her own.

In conclusion, for graphic designers like Lisa, AI, and ChatGPT can serve as invaluable tools for trend analysis and adaptation. By following the principles outlined in this chapter – from trendspotting to creative adaptation, fusion, testing, personalization, continuous updates, and ethical considerations – designers can ensure their work remains fresh and relevant in a rapidly changing design landscape.

Note: Please be aware that the strategies, tasks, and ideas discussed in this chapter can be further refined by taking advantage of ChatGPT's Advanced Data Analysis feature. If you require additional information about this tool, you can find comprehensive coverage in the previously authored chapter.

Task: Trend Research

ChatGPT can help gather information on current design trends in various industries and demographics.

Example Prompt 1:
Create a prompt to gather insights on the latest design trends in the fashion industry, focusing on color palettes, patterns, and

typography preferences among different age groups and regions.

Example Prompt 2:
Develop a prompt to analyze the emerging design trends in the technology sector, including user interface preferences, graphic styles, and branding elements across different global markets.

Example Prompt 3:
Craft a prompt to explore the current design trends in the home decor and interior design industry, covering popular themes, materials, and visual aesthetics favored by different socioeconomic demographics.

Example Prompt 4:
Design a prompt to investigate the evolving design trends in the food and beverage industry, including packaging designs, logo styles, and visual storytelling approaches that resonate with diverse consumer segments.

Task: Competitive Analysis

ChatGPT can assist in analyzing the design strategies of competitors and identifying successful trends.

Example Prompt 1:
Utilize ChatGPT's advanced data processing functionality to analyze and compare the design strategies of top competitors in the industry. Identify common trends and successful elements in their visual branding and user interface design.

Example Prompt 2:
Use ChatGPT to gather and process data on the color schemes, typography, and layout choices of key competitors. Identify any patterns or successful design strategies that can be incorporated into our own brand's visual identity.

Example Prompt 3:
Leverage ChatGPT's advanced data processing capabilities to analyze user feedback and reviews on competitor's design

elements. Identify which design features are resonating with users and contributing to a positive user experience.

Example Prompt 4:
Employ ChatGPT to analyze and compare the use of imagery, iconography, and visual storytelling in the design strategies of competitors. Identify any successful trends or storytelling techniques that can be adapted for our own brand's design approach.

Task: Consumer Behavior Analysis

ChatGPT can provide insights into consumer preferences and behaviors related to design trends.

Example Prompt 1:
Utilize ChatGPT's advanced data processing functionality to analyze consumer chat logs and social media interactions to identify emerging design trends and preferences among different demographic groups.

Example Prompt 2:
Use ChatGPT to analyze customer feedback and reviews to understand how design elements impact consumer behavior and purchasing decisions.

Example Prompt 3:
Leverage ChatGPT's data processing capabilities to track and analyze consumer engagement with different design styles and aesthetics across various online platforms and e-commerce websites.

Example Prompt 4:
Employ ChatGPT's advanced data processing functionality to conduct sentiment analysis on consumer conversations and interactions related to design trends, providing insights into the emotional impact of different design elements on consumer behavior.

Task: Trend Forecasting

ChatGPT can help predict future design trends based on current patterns and market indicators.

Example Prompt 1:
Analyze current design trends in the fashion industry and predict potential future trends based on consumer behavior and social media engagement using ChatGPT's advanced data processing functionality.

Example Prompt 2:
Utilize ChatGPT's data processing capabilities to analyze patterns in color usage and design elements across various industries, and forecast potential future trends in graphic design and branding.

Example Prompt 3:
Use ChatGPT's advanced data processing to analyze market indicators and consumer preferences in home decor and interior design, and predict upcoming trends in furniture and decor styles.

Example Prompt 4:
Leverage ChatGPT's data processing functionality to analyze patterns in website and app design, and forecast potential future trends in user interface and user experience design.

Task: Adaptation Strategies

ChatGPT can suggest ways to adapt current designs to align with popular trends.

Example Prompt 1:
Analyze current design trends in the graphic design industry and suggest specific adaptations to align with these trends.

Example Prompt 2:
Utilize ChatGPT's advanced data processing to identify emerging color palettes, typography styles, and visual elements that can be

incorporated into existing designs.

Example Prompt 3:
Provide insights on how to adapt designs to cater to specific target audiences or demographics based on current market trends and preferences.

Example Prompt 4:
Use ChatGPT's data processing capabilities to analyze competitor designs and suggest adaptations to stay competitive and relevant in the market.

Task: Design Trend Presentation

ChatGPT can assist in creating visual and written presentations on design trends for clients or team members.

Example Prompt 1:
Create a visual presentation showcasing the latest design trends in web and app interfaces, using ChatGPT's advanced data processing to analyze and summarize industry reports and articles.

Example Prompt 2:
Utilize ChatGPT's advanced data processing to gather and analyze data on color and typography trends in graphic design, and create a visually appealing presentation to showcase these trends.

Example Prompt 3:
Compile a written and visual presentation on emerging design trends in packaging and branding, using ChatGPT's advanced data processing to summarize market research and consumer behavior data.

Example Prompt 4:
Use ChatGPT's advanced data processing to analyze and summarize data on sustainable design trends, and create a presentation highlighting eco-friendly materials and design practices in the industry.

Idea: Trend Analysis Infographics

Create visually appealing infographics that showcase the latest design trends in various industries.

Example Prompt 1:

Hey ChatGPT, as a graphic designer, I need your help to analyze the latest design trends in the fashion industry and create an infographic that visually showcases the key trends. Can you process the data and provide me with insights to create a visually appealing trend analysis infographic?

Example Prompt 2:

ChatGPT, I'm looking to create an infographic that highlights the emerging design trends in the technology sector. Can you assist me in processing the data to identify the key trends and provide insights that I can use to design a visually appealing infographic?

Example Prompt 3:

As a graphic designer, I want to create an infographic that showcases the current design trends in the automotive industry. Can you help me analyze the data and provide insights that will allow me to create a visually appealing and informative trend analysis infographic?

Example Prompt 4:

ChatGPT, I'm working on a project to create infographics that illustrate the latest design trends in the home decor and interior design industry. Can you support me in processing the data to identify the trends and provide insights that will help me design visually appealing infographics for this sector?

Idea: Trend Adaptation Social Media Posts

Design social media posts that demonstrate how your business is adapting to current design trends.

Example Prompt 1:

ChatGPT, analyze current design trends in social media posts and create a series of social media posts for our business that demonstrate how we are adapting to these trends. Incorporate elements such as minimalist design, bold typography, and vibrant color schemes.

Example Prompt 2:
Utilizing ChatGPT's advanced data processing, research the latest design trends in social media posts and develop a set of visually appealing posts that showcase our business's adaptation to these trends. Focus on incorporating elements such as animated graphics, interactive elements, and immersive storytelling.

Example Prompt 3:
ChatGPT, leverage advanced data processing to identify emerging design trends in social media posts and create a collection of visually striking posts that highlight our business's innovative approach to design. Emphasize elements such as 3D graphics, augmented reality features, and seamless integration of multimedia content.

Example Prompt 4:
Harnessing ChatGPT's advanced data processing capabilities, analyze the evolving landscape of design trends in social media posts and craft a series of engaging posts that illustrate our business's commitment to staying ahead of the curve. Incorporate elements such as micro-animations, dynamic layouts, and personalized user experiences.

Idea: Trend Analysis Webinars

Host webinars discussing the latest design trends and how they can be incorporated into graphic design projects.

Example Prompt 1:
ChatGPT, analyze the latest design trends in graphic design and provide insights on how they can be incorporated into projects. Use the data to create a presentation for a webinar on trend analysis in

graphic design.

Example Prompt 2:
ChatGPT, gather data on the most popular design trends in the industry and create a report that can be used as a basis for hosting webinars discussing the latest design trends and their impact on graphic design projects.

Example Prompt 3:
ChatGPT, analyze social media and industry publications to identify the current design trends. Use this data to develop a webinar series that explores the latest trends and how they can be applied in graphic design projects.

Example Prompt 4:
ChatGPT, utilize advanced data processing to track and analyze the evolution of design trends over time. Use this information to create a series of webinars that delve into the history and future of design trends in graphic design.

Idea: Trend Adaptation Case Studies

Create case studies showcasing how your business has successfully adapted to recent design trends in client projects.

Example Prompt 1:
Prompt: "ChatGPT, analyze our client project data and identify recent design trends that have been successfully incorporated. Create case studies showcasing how our business has adapted to these trends and the impact it has had on client projects."

Example Prompt 2:
Prompt: "Utilize ChatGPT's advanced data processing to identify emerging design trends in the industry. Then, create case studies highlighting how our business has effectively integrated these trends into our client projects, showcasing the successful adaptation to current design trends."

Example Prompt 3:

Prompt: "ChatGPT, analyze our client project data to identify the most prominent design trends that have emerged in the past year. Use this information to create case studies demonstrating how our business has successfully adapted to these trends in our client projects, showcasing our ability to stay ahead of design trends."

Example Prompt 4:
Prompt: "Leverage ChatGPT's advanced data processing capabilities to analyze our client project data and identify the most impactful design trends that have influenced our work. Then, create case studies showcasing how our business has effectively adapted to these trends, providing real-world examples of our successful trend adaptation in client projects."

Idea: Trend Analysis Email Campaigns
Design visually engaging email campaigns that highlight the importance of trend analysis in graphic design.

Example Prompt 1:
ChatGPT, analyze current design trends in the graphic design industry and create visually engaging email campaign templates that showcase the importance of trend analysis in graphic design.

Example Prompt 2:
Utilize ChatGPT's advanced data processing capabilities to identify emerging design trends and incorporate them into visually appealing email campaign designs that emphasize the significance of trend analysis in graphic design.

Example Prompt 3:
Leverage ChatGPT's data processing functionality to gather insights on the latest design trends and use this information to develop compelling email campaign visuals that communicate the value of trend analysis in graphic design.

Example Prompt 4:
Task ChatGPT with analyzing market data and design trends to

inform the creation of visually captivating email campaigns that underscore the critical role of trend analysis in graphic design.

Idea: Trend Adaptation Portfolio Updates

Update your portfolio with projects that demonstrate your ability to adapt to current design trends.

Example Prompt 1:
ChatGPT, analyze current design trends in the graphic design industry and suggest project ideas that showcase my ability to adapt to these trends for my portfolio update.

Example Prompt 2:
ChatGPT, utilize advanced data processing to gather information on the latest design trends and provide me with a list of potential projects to include in my portfolio that align with these trends.

Example Prompt 3:
ChatGPT, help me identify the most relevant and impactful design trends in the industry and recommend specific projects from my portfolio that best demonstrate my ability to adapt to these trends.

Example Prompt 4:
ChatGPT, use advanced data processing to analyze the evolution of design trends over the past year and suggest updates to my portfolio that reflect my ability to stay current and adapt to these changes.

Idea: Trend Analysis Blog Posts

Write blog posts discussing the significance of trend analysis in graphic design and how it impacts businesses.

Example Prompt 1:
ChatGPT, analyze current trends in graphic design and provide insights on how these trends impact businesses. Use the data to create a blog post discussing the significance of trend analysis in graphic design.

Example Prompt 2:
Utilize ChatGPT's advanced data processing capabilities to gather information on the latest trends in graphic design. Then, craft a blog post that delves into the importance of trend analysis and its influence on businesses within the design industry.

Example Prompt 3:
Task ChatGPT with conducting a comprehensive trend analysis within the graphic design field. Use the findings to write a blog post that explores the impact of these trends on businesses and the significance of trend analysis in the design industry.

Example Prompt 4:
Employ ChatGPT's advanced data processing functionality to research and analyze current trends in graphic design. Leverage the insights to create a blog post that highlights the importance of trend analysis in graphic design and its implications for businesses.

Idea: Trend Adaptation Client Workshops

Offer workshops to clients on how they can adapt their branding and design to current trends.

Example Prompt 1:
ChatGPT, can you analyze current design and branding trends in the market and provide a comprehensive report for our Trend Adaptation Client Workshops?

Example Prompt 2:
Please use ChatGPT's advanced data processing to gather insights on the latest design and branding trends, and create a presentation for our Trend Adaptation Client Workshops.

Example Prompt 3:
Utilize ChatGPT's data processing capabilities to identify key visual elements and color schemes that are trending, and incorporate them into our Trend Adaptation Client Workshop

materials.

Example Prompt 4:

We need ChatGPT to help us analyze consumer behavior and preferences in design, so we can tailor our Trend Adaptation Client Workshops to meet their needs effectively.

Idea: Trend Analysis Trend Reports

Create visually appealing trend reports that outline the latest design trends and how they can be applied in graphic design.

Example Prompt 1:

Hey ChatGPT, I need your help to analyze the latest design trends and create visually appealing trend reports for graphic design. Can you gather data on the most popular design styles, color palettes, and typography trends, and present them in a visually engaging format?

Example Prompt 2:

ChatGPT, I'm looking to stay ahead of the curve in graphic design. Can you use your advanced data processing functionality to analyze current design trends and help me create trend reports that showcase the latest developments in the industry?

Example Prompt 3:

As a graphic designer, I want to understand the latest design trends and how they can be applied in my work. ChatGPT, can you assist me in compiling trend reports that highlight the most influential design movements and present them in a visually appealing format?

Example Prompt 4:

I'm seeking to create trend reports that outline the latest design trends and their impact on graphic design. ChatGPT, can you help me analyze data on emerging design styles and present the findings in visually engaging reports that I can use for inspiration in my work?

Idea: Trend Adaptation Branding Guides

Develop branding guides for clients that incorporate current design trends and demonstrate their adaptability.

Example Prompt 1:
ChatGPT, using advanced data processing, create branding guides for our clients that showcase their adaptability to current design trends. Include examples of how their brand can evolve to stay relevant in the ever-changing market.

Example Prompt 2:
Utilizing ChatGPT's advanced data processing capabilities, develop branding guides for our clients that highlight their ability to incorporate and adapt to the latest design trends. Show how their brand can remain fresh and appealing to their target audience.

Example Prompt 3:
ChatGPT, with its advanced data processing functionality, support us in creating branding guides for our clients that emphasize their flexibility and responsiveness to current design trends. Provide visual examples and strategies for maintaining a modern and adaptable brand image.

Example Prompt 4:
We need ChatGPT to utilize its advanced data processing capabilities to craft branding guides for our clients that demonstrate their ability to seamlessly integrate current design trends. Show how their brand can stay relevant and adaptable in a fast-paced market.

Idea: Trend Analysis Video Content

Produce video content that visually showcases the latest design trends and how they can be utilized in graphic design projects.

Example Prompt 1:

Hey ChatGPT, I need your help to analyze the latest design trends in graphic design and create a visually engaging video showcasing how these trends can be utilized in projects. Can you process the data to identify the top 5 design trends and provide examples of how they can be incorporated into various graphic design projects?

Example Prompt 2:

ChatGPT, I'm looking to create a trend analysis video for graphic design, highlighting the latest design trends and their applications. Can you use your advanced data processing capabilities to gather information on the current design trends and provide insights on how they can be visually represented in a video content?

Example Prompt 3:

As a graphic designer, I want to produce a video that showcases the latest design trends and their practical applications in graphic design projects. Can you assist me in processing data to identify the most relevant trends and provide visual examples of how they can be integrated into design projects?

Example Prompt 4:

I'm seeking to create a video content that visually presents the latest design trends and their potential impact on graphic design projects. ChatGPT, can you utilize your advanced data processing functionality to analyze the current design trends and help me illustrate their application in a compelling video?

Idea: Trend Adaptation Interactive Presentations

Design interactive presentations that demonstrate how your business is adapting to current design trends and how it can benefit clients.

Example Prompt 1:

Prompt: "ChatGPT, create an interactive presentation showcasing our business's adaptation to current design trends, including examples of how these trends benefit our clients. Utilize advanced data processing to incorporate real-time trend data and visually demonstrate our innovative approach."

Example Prompt 2:

Prompt: "ChatGPT, develop a dynamic presentation that highlights our company's responsiveness to evolving design trends. Use advanced data processing to analyze industry trends and create interactive visualizations that illustrate our adaptation strategy and its potential impact on client projects."

Example Prompt 3:

Prompt: "ChatGPT, assist in crafting an interactive presentation that communicates our business's agility in embracing design trends. Leverage advanced data processing to integrate trend analysis and create engaging visual content that showcases our ability to stay ahead of the curve and deliver value to our clients."

Example Prompt 4:

Prompt: "ChatGPT, help us build an interactive presentation that showcases our business's commitment to staying current with design trends. Utilize advanced data processing to incorporate trend data and create interactive elements that demonstrate how our adaptation to trends can enhance the creative solutions we offer to our clients."

CLIENT COMMUNICATION AND NEGOTIATION

DESIGN DIALOGUES: EFFECTIVE CLIENT COMMUNICATION

In the world of graphic design, effective client communication and negotiation skills are as crucial as your design abilities. Let's follow the journey of Alex, a skilled graphic designer, as he leverages the power of artificial intelligence, specifically ChatGPT, to navigate these critical aspects of the profession.

Understanding Client Needs:

Alex begins by using AI to conduct in-depth research on his clients and their industries. ChatGPT assists him in understanding their pain points, target audience, and competitors, enabling him to tailor his design proposals to meet their specific needs.

Clear and Concise Communication:

AI-powered chatbots, driven by ChatGPT's natural language processing capabilities, help Alex maintain clear and prompt communication with his clients. Automated responses to routine queries free up his time for more meaningful interactions.

Visual Prototyping:

Alex employs AI-assisted design tools to create rapid prototypes. ChatGPT generates design descriptions and rationale, making it easier for clients to visualize the final product. This visual communication fosters a deeper understanding of design concepts.

Negotiation and Value Proposition:

Before diving into project terms, Alex uses AI-generated market insights to establish the value of his design services. He negotiates with confidence, backed by data-driven arguments, ensuring a fair deal for both parties.

Transparency and Collaboration:

Alex maintains transparency throughout the design process, using AI to provide real-time progress updates and share design iterations with clients. ChatGPT assists in facilitating collaborative feedback, fostering a sense of partnership.

Conflict Resolution:

In the rare event of disagreements, ChatGPT helps Alex navigate difficult conversations. It suggests diplomatic language and alternative solutions, allowing him to resolve conflicts professionally and maintain strong client relationships.

Personalization and Customization:

Alex tailors his communication style to each client, thanks to AI's ability to analyze their communication preferences.

Whether it's email, video calls, or chat, he adapts to ensure clients feel heard and understood.

By incorporating artificial intelligence into his client communication and negotiation strategies, Alex ensures a smoother and more productive working relationship with his clients. He combines his design expertise with AI-driven insights to provide solutions that exceed client expectations.

In conclusion, for graphic designers like Alex, artificial intelligence and ChatGPT serve as invaluable tools for effective client communication and negotiation. By following the principles outlined in this chapter – from understanding client needs to clear communication, visual prototyping, data-backed negotiation, transparency, conflict resolution, and personalization – designers can foster strong client relationships and secure successful projects in the dynamic world of graphic design.

Task: Initial client inquiry

Responding to initial client inquiries and requests for information about your services

Example Prompt 1:
Hello! Thank you for reaching out about my graphic design services. Can you provide me with some details about the project you have in mind? This will help me better understand your needs and provide you with an accurate quote.

Example Prompt 2:
Hi there! I'm glad to hear that you're interested in my graphic design services. Could you tell me a bit about your business and the specific design needs you have? This will help me tailor my services to best meet your requirements.

Example Prompt 3:

Hello and thank you for considering my graphic design services. To better assist you, could you provide me with some information about your timeline and budget for this project? This will help me determine the best approach to meeting your needs.

Example Prompt 4:

Hi! I'm excited to discuss your graphic design needs. Can you share any specific design ideas or inspirations you have in mind? This will help me understand your vision and create a design that aligns with your expectations.

Task: Project scope clarification

Clarifying the scope of the project and discussing the client's specific needs and expectations

Example Prompt 1:

Can you provide more details about the specific goals and objectives of the project? This will help us understand the scope and deliverables more clearly.

Example Prompt 2:

What are the key elements or features that you envision for this project? Understanding your specific needs will help us tailor our design approach accordingly.

Example Prompt 3:

Could you share any examples or references that capture the aesthetic or style you're aiming for? This will give us a better understanding of your expectations and preferences.

Example Prompt 4:

Are there any specific constraints or limitations that we should be aware of when defining the scope of the project? This could include budget, timeline, or technical requirements.

Task: Setting project timelines

Negotiating project timelines and deadlines with the client

Example Prompt 1:

How do you typically set project timelines for your design projects? Are there any specific factors or considerations that you take into account when determining deadlines?

Example Prompt 2:

When negotiating project timelines with a client, what strategies do you find most effective in ensuring that both parties are satisfied with the proposed deadlines?

Example Prompt 3:

Can you share any tips or best practices for effectively communicating project timelines and deadlines to clients in a way that fosters understanding and collaboration?

Example Prompt 4:

In your experience as a graphic designer, how do you handle situations where clients request unrealistic project timelines? What approach do you take to negotiate more feasible deadlines while maintaining the quality of your work?

Task: Budget negotiation

Discussing and negotiating the budget for the project

Example Prompt 1:

How can we align our budget expectations to ensure we can deliver a high-quality design project within the allocated resources?

Example Prompt 2:

Let's discuss the specific elements of the project that are most important to allocate budget towards, and how we can optimize our resources for maximum impact.

Example Prompt 3:

What are the key factors influencing the budget for this project, and how can we work together to find a solution that meets both our design needs and budget constraints?

Example Prompt 4:
In what ways can we creatively approach budget negotiation to ensure we can achieve our design goals while staying within the agreed-upon financial parameters?

Task: Revisions and feedback

Managing client feedback and negotiating the number of revisions included in the project scope

Example Prompt 1:
How can we incorporate your feedback into the design to better align with your vision for the project?

Example Prompt 2:
What specific revisions would you like to see in the design, and how can we work together to ensure they are implemented effectively?

Example Prompt 3:
Let's discuss the number of revisions included in the project scope and how we can best manage additional revisions that may arise during the design process.

Example Prompt 4:
What are your expectations for the revision process, and how can we ensure that we meet those expectations while staying within the project scope?

Task: Contract negotiation

Negotiating the terms of the contract and ensuring both parties are in agreement

Example Prompt 1:
Can you provide a breakdown of the specific deliverables and

timelines outlined in the contract to ensure we are both on the same page?

Example Prompt 2:
Let's discuss the payment terms and schedule to ensure it aligns with both of our expectations and needs.

Example Prompt 3:
Are there any specific clauses or provisions that you feel are essential to include in the contract for the protection of both parties?

Example Prompt 4:
How do you envision handling any potential changes or amendments to the contract during the course of our working relationship?

Task: Handling client objections

Addressing any objections or concerns the client may have about the project

Example Prompt 1:
How can we address any concerns or objections you may have about the design direction or concept for this project?

Example Prompt 2:
What specific objections or concerns do you have about the proposed design, and how can we work together to find a solution?

Example Prompt 3:
In what ways can we adjust the design to better meet your needs and address any objections you may have?

Example Prompt 4:
Let's discuss any objections or concerns you have about the project, and brainstorm potential solutions to ensure your satisfaction with the final design.

Task: Managing client expectations

Communicating realistic expectations and managing any potential misunderstandings

Example Prompt 1:
How can we effectively communicate the timeline and process for this project to ensure that our client's expectations are realistic and manageable?

Example Prompt 2:
What strategies can we use to set clear boundaries and limitations with our clients in order to avoid any potential misunderstandings about the scope of the project?

Example Prompt 3:
In what ways can we utilize visual aids and mockups to help clients better understand the design process and manage their expectations for the final product?

Example Prompt 4:
What are some effective techniques for addressing and managing client feedback in a way that aligns with their expectations and ensures a smooth design process?

Task: Final project delivery

Negotiating the final delivery of the project and ensuring the client is satisfied with the outcome

Example Prompt 1:
How can we ensure that the final project delivery meets all of your expectations and requirements? Let's discuss any specific details or adjustments you may need to make sure you are completely satisfied with the outcome.

Example Prompt 2:
What are your thoughts on the current state of the project? Are

there any final touches or revisions you would like to see before we consider it complete?

Example Prompt 3:
Let's go over the final project delivery timeline and make sure it aligns with your expectations. Are there any specific deadlines or milestones we need to keep in mind as we finalize the project?

Example Prompt 4:
In order to ensure your satisfaction with the final delivery, let's discuss any potential changes or additions you would like to see. Your feedback is crucial in making sure the project meets your needs and vision.

Idea: Client Communication Templates

ChatGPT can help create email templates for initial client outreach, project updates, and follow-up communications.

Example Prompt 1:
Create a set of email templates for initial client outreach, including a friendly introduction, a brief overview of services, and a call to action for scheduling a meeting or call.

Example Prompt 2:
Design a series of project update email templates, including progress reports, milestone achievements, and any necessary requests for client feedback or input.

Example Prompt 3:
Develop a set of follow-up communication templates, including thank you notes, check-in emails, and requests for client testimonials or referrals.

Example Prompt 4:
Design visually appealing email templates that align with our brand identity and can be easily customized with client-specific details for a personalized touch.

Idea: Negotiation Strategies

ChatGPT can provide tips and strategies for negotiating project terms, pricing, and timelines with clients.

Example Prompt 1:
Design a series of visually appealing infographics that illustrate effective negotiation strategies for project terms, pricing, and timelines with clients. Include key tips and tactics for successful negotiations.

Example Prompt 2:
Create a set of eye-catching social media graphics that highlight the importance of clear communication and assertiveness in negotiating project terms, pricing, and timelines with clients. Use engaging visuals and concise messaging to convey the message effectively.

Example Prompt 3:
Develop a visually engaging presentation deck that outlines various negotiation strategies for project terms, pricing, and timelines with clients. Incorporate relevant images, charts, and diagrams to support the key points and make the content more engaging.

Example Prompt 4:
Design a visually appealing e-book cover and layout for a guide on negotiation strategies specifically tailored to the creative industry. The design should be modern, professional, and reflective of the valuable content within, focusing on project terms, pricing, and timelines negotiation.

Idea: Client Questionnaires

ChatGPT can assist in creating questionnaires to gather important information from clients about their design needs and preferences.

Example Prompt 1:

Create a client questionnaire template that can be used to gather information about a client's design preferences, including color schemes, style preferences, and specific design elements they are drawn to.

Example Prompt 2:

Assist in developing a series of open-ended questions that can be used to gather detailed information from clients about their design needs, such as their target audience, brand identity, and design goals.

Example Prompt 3:

Design a visually appealing and user-friendly questionnaire layout that can be easily shared with clients and completed online, ensuring a seamless experience for gathering design preferences and requirements.

Example Prompt 4:

Help in creating a customizable questionnaire that can be tailored to different design projects, allowing for specific questions related to website design, branding, packaging, or other design needs.

Idea: Communication Best Practices

ChatGPT can provide guidance on effective communication methods and best practices for maintaining a positive client relationship.

Example Prompt 1:

Can you provide tips on how to effectively communicate with clients to build a strong and positive relationship?

Example Prompt 2:

I need guidance on the best practices for maintaining clear and professional communication with clients. Can you help with that?

Example Prompt 3:

As a graphic designer, I want to ensure I am effectively communicating with my clients. Can you provide advice on the best methods for doing so?

Example Prompt 4:
I'm looking for tips on how to improve my client communication skills and maintain a positive relationship. Can you offer some guidance on this?

Idea: Setting Expectations

ChatGPT can help craft messages that clearly outline project expectations, deliverables, and timelines to clients.

Example Prompt 1:
Design a visually appealing template for a project proposal that clearly outlines project expectations, deliverables, and timelines for clients.

Example Prompt 2:
Create a series of infographics that visually represent the different stages of a project, including expectations, deliverables, and timelines, to help clients better understand the process.

Example Prompt 3:
Develop a set of customizable email templates that can be used to communicate project expectations, deliverables, and timelines to clients in a clear and professional manner.

Example Prompt 4:
Design a visually engaging presentation template that can be used to present project expectations, deliverables, and timelines to clients during meetings or pitches.

Idea: Handling Difficult Clients

ChatGPT can offer advice on how to navigate challenging client interactions and maintain professionalism.

Example Prompt 1:
As a graphic designer, I often encounter difficult clients who have unrealistic expectations. Can ChatGPT provide tips on how to handle these situations and maintain professionalism throughout the process?

Example Prompt 2:
I'm struggling with a client who keeps making last-minute changes to the design project, causing delays and frustration. Can ChatGPT offer advice on how to effectively communicate boundaries and manage these difficult client interactions?

Example Prompt 3:
Dealing with demanding clients can be overwhelming at times. Can ChatGPT provide strategies for setting clear expectations, managing feedback, and maintaining a positive working relationship with challenging clients?

Example Prompt 4:
I need help navigating a difficult client who is constantly micromanaging the design process. Can ChatGPT offer guidance on how to assert boundaries, maintain creative control, and handle challenging client interactions with professionalism?

Idea: Pricing Negotiation Tips

ChatGPT can provide insights on how to negotiate pricing with clients while maintaining the value of your design services.

Example Prompt 1:
Prompt: "Hey ChatGPT, can you provide some strategies for negotiating pricing with clients in the graphic design industry? I want to ensure that I am able to maintain the value of my design services while also being fair to my clients."

Example Prompt 2:
Prompt: "ChatGPT, I'm looking for some advice on how to

handle pricing negotiations with potential clients for my graphic design services. Can you provide some tips on how to effectively communicate the value of my work while also being open to negotiation?"

Example Prompt 3:

Prompt: "I'm in need of some guidance on negotiating pricing for my graphic design services. ChatGPT, can you offer some insights on how to approach these discussions with clients in a way that maintains the value of my work while also being flexible in meeting their budget?"

Example Prompt 4:

Prompt: "ChatGPT, I'm seeking some support in navigating pricing negotiations with clients for my graphic design work. Can you provide some tips on how to effectively communicate the worth of my services and find a mutually beneficial pricing agreement?"

Idea: Client Feedback Forms

ChatGPT can assist in creating feedback forms to gather input from clients on design drafts and revisions.

Example Prompt 1:

Prompt: "Create a client feedback form template for design drafts and revisions. Include questions about overall satisfaction, specific design elements, and suggestions for improvement. The form should be visually appealing and easy to navigate."

Example Prompt 2:

Prompt: "Design a series of feedback form options for different design projects, such as logos, websites, and marketing materials. Each form should be tailored to gather specific input related to the type of project and should reflect the branding of the client."

Example Prompt 3:

Prompt: "Develop a digital feedback form that can be easily integrated into email communications or project management platforms. The form should allow for file uploads, so clients can provide visual examples or references for their feedback."

Example Prompt 4:
Prompt: "Create a visually engaging infographic or presentation summarizing the feedback gathered from clients on design drafts and revisions. The visual representation should highlight key trends and insights to inform future design decisions."

Idea: Contract Negotiation

ChatGPT can provide guidance on negotiating contract terms and ensuring legal protection for your design work.

Example Prompt 1:
Hey ChatGPT, can you provide tips on negotiating contract terms for graphic design projects? I want to ensure legal protection for my work.

Example Prompt 2:
I need help understanding how to negotiate contracts for my graphic design services. Can ChatGPT provide guidance on this?

Example Prompt 3:
ChatGPT, can you assist me in understanding the legal aspects of contract negotiation for graphic design work? I want to make sure my designs are protected.

Example Prompt 4:
I'm looking for advice on negotiating contracts for my graphic design business. Can ChatGPT help me understand the legal implications and how to protect my work?

Idea: Client Education Materials

ChatGPT can help create educational materials to inform clients about the design process and the value of your services.

Example Prompt 1:

Create a series of infographics explaining the different stages of the design process, from initial concept to final delivery, to help clients understand the value of your services.

Example Prompt 2:
Develop a chatbot script that can interact with clients and provide them with information about the importance of good design and how it can benefit their business.

Example Prompt 3:
Design a visually appealing presentation that outlines the various design services you offer and the impact they can have on a client's brand and marketing efforts.

Example Prompt 4:
Produce a set of interactive tutorials or videos that walk clients through the design process, showcasing the expertise and attention to detail that goes into each project.

Idea: Conflict Resolution Strategies

ChatGPT can offer advice on resolving conflicts with clients in a professional and amicable manner.

Example Prompt 1:
Can you provide a step-by-step guide on how to de-escalate a conflict with a client and reach a mutually beneficial resolution?

Example Prompt 2:
I need some visual aids or infographics that illustrate effective communication techniques for diffusing tense situations with clients. Can you create those for me?

Example Prompt 3:
I'm looking for a series of social media graphics that convey the importance of active listening and empathy in resolving conflicts with clients. Can you design those for me?

Example Prompt 4:

I'd like to create a digital booklet or brochure outlining different conflict resolution strategies for client-facing professionals. Can you help me design the layout and visuals for this project?

Idea: Client Retention Strategies

ChatGPT can provide ideas for maintaining long-term relationships with clients and fostering repeat business.

Example Prompt 1:
As a graphic designer, I need help brainstorming creative ways to incorporate client retention strategies into my client communication materials. Can ChatGPT provide ideas for designing visually appealing newsletters, email campaigns, or social media graphics that will help maintain long-term relationships with clients?

Example Prompt 2:
I'm looking for innovative design concepts to create a client loyalty program that will keep customers coming back for more. Can ChatGPT suggest visually engaging and effective ways to design loyalty cards, promotional materials, or digital rewards that will foster repeat business and enhance client retention?

Example Prompt 3:
I want to revamp my client onboarding process with visually captivating materials that will leave a lasting impression and encourage long-term relationships. Can ChatGPT provide design ideas for welcome kits, client welcome packages, or personalized onboarding materials that will help retain clients and build loyalty?

Example Prompt 4:
I'm seeking visually appealing ways to showcase client success stories and testimonials to demonstrate the value of our services and encourage repeat business. Can ChatGPT suggest design concepts for creating client testimonial videos, case study infographics, or client success story presentations that will help

maintain long-term relationships with clients?

ETHICAL DESIGN AND ACCESSIBILITY

DESIGN WITH A CONSCIENCE: ETHICS AND ACCESSIBILITY

In the realm of graphic design, ethics and accessibility are non-negotiable facets of responsible practice. Let's follow the journey of Maya, a conscientious graphic designer, as she integrates artificial intelligence, specifically ChatGPT, into her design process while championing ethical design and accessibility.

User-Centered Ethical Design:

Maya begins by recognizing that ethical design starts with putting the user first. AI-driven sentiment analysis by ChatGPT helps her gauge public perception, ensuring that her designs align with societal values and avoid inadvertently causing harm or offense.

Inclusive Accessibility:

Maya embraces the principle that her designs should be accessible to all. ChatGPT provides her with accessibility guidelines and suggests alternative text for images, enabling her to create content that can be experienced by users with disabilities.

Diversity and Representation:

Maya understands the importance of diverse representation in her designs. AI-powered demographic analysis tools assist her in understanding her target audience's composition, ensuring her designs are inclusive and relatable to a broad range of people.

AI-Powered Auditing:

Before finalizing her designs, Maya employs AI-driven accessibility auditing tools. ChatGPT identifies potential issues and offers solutions, ensuring her work complies with accessibility standards.

Ethical Data Usage:

Maya ensures she ethically sources and handles any data used in her designs. She uses AI to anonymize and protect user data, maintaining their privacy and trust.

Community Involvement:

Maya actively engages with the design community and participates in discussions on ethical design and accessibility. ChatGPT helps her stay updated on industry standards and best practices.

User Feedback and Iteration:

Maya encourages user feedback and uses sentiment analysis powered by ChatGPT to understand their experiences. She iterates her designs based on this feedback, continuously striving to improve accessibility and ethical considerations.

By combining the power of artificial intelligence with her commitment to ethical design and accessibility, Maya ensures her work not only meets high standards but also positively impacts users from all walks of life.

In conclusion, for graphic designers like Maya, the integration of AI tools like ChatGPT is a powerful ally in promoting ethical design and accessibility. By following the principles outlined in this chapter – user-centered ethics, inclusive accessibility, diversity, AI-powered auditing, ethical data usage, community involvement, and user feedback – designers can create content that not only looks good but also contributes to a more inclusive and ethical design landscape.

Task: Ethical design principles

Provide guidelines and best practices for creating designs that prioritize user well-being and respect ethical standards.

Example Prompt 1:
How can we ensure that our designs prioritize user well-being and respect ethical standards? What are some key ethical design principles to keep in mind?

Example Prompt 2:
What are some best practices for creating designs that prioritize user privacy and data security? How can we incorporate these principles into our graphic design work?

Example Prompt 3:
Can you provide examples of designs that successfully prioritize user well-being and respect ethical standards? What specific elements or techniques contribute to their ethical design?

Example Prompt 4:

In what ways can graphic designers advocate for and incorporate diversity, equity, and inclusion in their designs? What are some strategies for ensuring that our designs are respectful and inclusive of all users?

Task: Accessibility standards

Offer information on designing for accessibility, including color contrast, font size, and other considerations for users with disabilities.

Example Prompt 1:
Can you provide some tips on designing for color contrast to ensure accessibility for users with visual impairments?

Example Prompt 2:
How can we ensure that our font size and style are accessible for users with dyslexia or other reading disabilities?

Example Prompt 3:
What are some best practices for designing user interfaces to be accessible for individuals with motor impairments or limited dexterity?

Example Prompt 4:
Can you offer guidance on creating accessible designs for users with cognitive disabilities, such as clear navigation and simplified layouts?

Task: Inclusive design techniques

Suggest methods for creating designs that are inclusive and considerate of diverse audiences.

Example Prompt 1:
How can graphic design incorporate accessibility features to ensure that diverse audiences, including those with disabilities, can easily engage with the content?

Example Prompt 2:
What are some techniques for using diverse representation in graphic design to ensure that all audiences feel included and represented in the visual content?

Example Prompt 3:
Can you suggest methods for creating designs that are culturally sensitive and respectful of diverse backgrounds and perspectives?

Example Prompt 4:
How can graphic design be used to promote inclusivity and diversity, and what are some best practices for incorporating these values into visual communication?

Task: User experience (UX) research

Provide resources for conducting user research to understand the needs and preferences of different user groups.

Example Prompt 1:
Can you share any best practices or resources for conducting user interviews to gather insights on user needs and preferences?

Example Prompt 2:
What are some effective methods for gathering quantitative data on user behavior and preferences, and how can this data be used to inform UX design decisions?

Example Prompt 3:
How can personas and user journey mapping be used to better understand the needs and preferences of different user groups, and what tools or templates do you recommend for creating these?

Example Prompt 4:
What are some key considerations for conducting usability testing with diverse user groups, and how can the findings from these tests be used to improve the overall user experience?

Task: Design critique and feedback

Offer guidance on receiving and incorporating feedback to improve the ethical and accessible aspects of a design.

Example Prompt 1:
Can you provide feedback on the color contrast and readability of this design? I want to ensure it is accessible to all users, including those with visual impairments.

Example Prompt 2:
I'm looking for critique on the use of imagery in this design. How can I ensure that the visuals are inclusive and representative of diverse perspectives?

Example Prompt 3:
I'd like feedback on the typography choices in this design. How can I make sure the text is easily readable and complies with ethical design principles?

Example Prompt 4:
How can I incorporate feedback on the layout and navigation of this design to make it more user-friendly and accessible for all individuals?

Task: Compliance with legal regulations

Provide information on legal requirements related to accessibility and ethical design, such as ADA compliance for digital platforms.

Example Prompt 1:
Can you provide information on the legal requirements for digital platforms related to accessibility, such as ADA compliance and ethical design standards?

Example Prompt 2:
What are the key legal regulations that graphic designers need to

consider when creating digital content, particularly in terms of accessibility and ethical design?

Example Prompt 3:
How can graphic designers ensure compliance with ADA regulations and other legal requirements for accessibility in their digital designs?

Example Prompt 4:
What are some best practices for ensuring ethical and accessible design in accordance with legal regulations, particularly for digital platforms?

Idea: Inclusive Design Workshops

ChatGPT can provide resources and materials for conducting workshops on inclusive design, covering topics such as accessibility, diversity, and ethical considerations in design.

Example Prompt 1:
Create a presentation deck on the importance of inclusive design, including statistics, case studies, and best practices for incorporating accessibility, diversity, and ethical considerations in design.

Example Prompt 2:
Develop a series of interactive exercises and activities that can be used to engage workshop participants in discussions and hands-on learning about inclusive design principles.

Example Prompt 3:
Compile a list of recommended reading materials, articles, and online resources for further exploration of inclusive design, accessibility, diversity, and ethical considerations in design.

Example Prompt 4:
Design a set of visually engaging and informative handouts or infographics that can be used to reinforce key concepts and takeaways from the inclusive design workshops.

Idea: Accessible Design Templates

ChatGPT can assist in creating design templates that prioritize accessibility, such as color-contrast compliant templates and easy-to-read font choices.

Example Prompt 1:
Hey ChatGPT, can you help me create a design template that prioritizes accessibility? I'm looking for color-contrast compliant options and easy-to-read font choices for a website I'm working on.

Example Prompt 2:
ChatGPT, I need your assistance in developing an accessible design template. Can you provide suggestions for color combinations and font choices that are easy to read for individuals with visual impairments?

Example Prompt 3:
I'm in need of an accessible design template for a project I'm working on. ChatGPT, can you help me create a template that ensures color contrast compliance and uses fonts that are easy to read for all users?

Example Prompt 4:
ChatGPT, I'm looking to create an inclusive design template that prioritizes accessibility. Can you provide guidance on color-contrast compliant options and font choices that are accessible to all users?

Idea: Ethical Design Guidelines

ChatGPT can help in drafting ethical design guidelines for the business, covering topics like data privacy, user consent, and responsible design practices.

Example Prompt 1:
Hey ChatGPT, can you help me draft ethical design guidelines for our business? We need to cover topics like data privacy, user

consent, and responsible design practices to ensure our products and services are aligned with ethical standards.

Example Prompt 2:
ChatGPT, I need your assistance in creating a set of ethical design guidelines for our company. We want to prioritize data privacy, user consent, and responsible design practices to ensure our products are ethically designed.

Example Prompt 3:
I'm looking to develop ethical design guidelines for our business, and I could use ChatGPT's support in covering important topics like data privacy, user consent, and responsible design practices. Can you help me with this?

Example Prompt 4:
ChatGPT, I need your expertise in drafting ethical design guidelines for our company. We want to ensure that our design practices prioritize data privacy, user consent, and responsible design. Can you assist us with this?

Idea: Accessibility Audits

ChatGPT can support in conducting accessibility audits for existing designs, providing insights and recommendations for improving accessibility.

Example Prompt 1:
Prompt: "Hey ChatGPT, as a graphic designer, I need your help in conducting an accessibility audit for a website design. Can you provide insights and recommendations for improving accessibility, such as color contrast, text size, and navigation?"

Example Prompt 2:
Prompt: "ChatGPT, I'm working on a mobile app design and I want to ensure it's accessible to all users. Can you assist me in conducting an accessibility audit, including recommendations for making the interface more user-friendly for people with disabilities?"

Example Prompt 3:

Prompt: *"As a graphic designer, I'm passionate about creating inclusive designs. ChatGPT, can you help me in conducting an accessibility audit for a series of social media graphics? I'd like to ensure they are accessible to all users, including those with visual impairments."*

Example Prompt 4:

Prompt: *"ChatGPT, I'm working on a new website design and I want to prioritize accessibility. Can you support me in conducting an accessibility audit, providing recommendations for improving the design's accessibility features, such as alt text for images and keyboard navigation?"*

Idea: Inclusive Icon Sets

ChatGPT can aid in creating inclusive icon sets that represent a diverse range of people and abilities, promoting inclusivity in design.

Example Prompt 1:

Create a set of inclusive icon designs that represent a diverse range of people and abilities, ensuring that all individuals feel represented and included in visual communication.

Example Prompt 2:

Assist in developing a collection of icon sets that accurately depict individuals with various physical abilities, ethnicities, and gender identities, promoting diversity and inclusivity in design.

Example Prompt 3:

Support in the creation of inclusive icon sets that showcase a wide spectrum of ages, body types, and cultural backgrounds, fostering a sense of belonging and representation for all individuals.

Example Prompt 4:

Help in designing a series of inclusive icons that accurately portray individuals with different physical and cognitive abilities, ensuring that everyone feels seen and valued in visual communication.

Idea: Ethical Design Training Materials

ChatGPT can assist in developing training materials for designers on ethical design principles and best practices.

Example Prompt 1:
Can you help create a comprehensive guide on ethical design principles and best practices for graphic designers? This could include case studies, practical examples, and actionable steps to ensure ethical considerations are integrated into every design project.

Example Prompt 2:
I need support in developing a series of interactive workshops or webinars for graphic designers focused on ethical design. Can you assist in creating engaging content and exercises that will help designers understand and apply ethical principles in their work?

Example Prompt 3:
I'm looking to produce a set of visually appealing and informative infographics or posters that highlight key ethical design concepts. Can you help in designing these materials to effectively communicate the importance of ethical considerations in design?

Example Prompt 4:
I want to create a digital resource hub for designers to access information and tools related to ethical design. Can you assist in developing an online platform or interactive content that will serve as a valuable educational resource for designers seeking to integrate ethical principles into their work?

Idea: Accessible Infographics

ChatGPT can help in creating accessible infographics that are easy to understand for all users, including those with disabilities.

Example Prompt 1:
Create an infographic that uses high contrast colors and large, easy-to-read fonts to ensure accessibility for users with visual impairments. Include alt text for all images and graphics to provide a comprehensive experience for screen reader users.

Example Prompt 2:
Design an infographic that utilizes simple, clear language and includes audio descriptions for each visual element to cater to users with cognitive disabilities. Ensure that the information is presented in a logical and easy-to-follow format for all users.

Example Prompt 3:
Develop an infographic that incorporates tactile elements or 3D printing options for users with physical disabilities, allowing them to interact with the information in a tangible way. Consider the use of braille or embossed graphics for enhanced accessibility.

Example Prompt 4:
Produce an infographic that is compatible with assistive technologies such as screen readers, voice recognition software, and switch devices, ensuring that all users, regardless of their abilities, can access and understand the content effectively.

Idea: Ethical Design Consultations

ChatGPT can provide guidance on ethical design decisions, helping designers navigate complex ethical considerations in their work.

Example Prompt 1:
Can you provide guidance on how to incorporate inclusive and diverse imagery in our designs, while avoiding stereotypes and cultural appropriation?

Example Prompt 2:
I need help understanding how to create user-friendly interfaces

that prioritize user privacy and data security. Can you offer advice on ethical design principles for digital products?

Example Prompt 3:
I'm struggling with the ethical implications of using certain color schemes and visual elements in my designs. Can you assist me in making more responsible design choices?

Example Prompt 4:
I'm looking for support in understanding how to design products that are accessible to all users, including those with disabilities. Can you provide insights on ethical considerations for inclusive design?

Idea: Inclusive Color Palettes

ChatGPT can support in creating color palettes that are accessible to users with visual impairments, ensuring that designs are inclusive for all.

Example Prompt 1:
Prompt: "Hey ChatGPT, as a graphic designer, I need help creating inclusive color palettes for my designs. Can you assist in generating color combinations that are accessible to users with visual impairments, ensuring that my designs are inclusive for all?"

Example Prompt 2:
Prompt: "ChatGPT, I'm working on a project that requires inclusive color palettes for users with visual impairments. Can you help me generate color schemes that are both aesthetically pleasing and accessible to all?"

Example Prompt 3:
Prompt: "As a graphic designer, I want to ensure that my color palettes are inclusive for all users, including those with visual impairments. Can ChatGPT help me create color combinations that are both visually appealing and accessible?"

Example Prompt 4:

Prompt: "ChatGPT, I'm looking to create inclusive color palettes for my designs to ensure accessibility for users with visual impairments. Can you provide assistance in generating color schemes that are both inclusive and visually engaging?"

Idea: Ethical Design Case Studies

ChatGPT can help in researching and compiling case studies that highlight the impact of ethical design choices on user experience and business success.

Example Prompt 1:

Can you help me research and compile case studies that showcase the positive impact of ethical design choices on user experience and business success? I'm looking to create a collection of examples to demonstrate the importance of ethical design in the industry.

Example Prompt 2:

I'm interested in exploring how ethical design choices have influenced user experience and business success in various industries. Can you assist me in finding and analyzing case studies that illustrate the impact of ethical design on different companies and their customers?

Example Prompt 3:

I'm looking to create a series of case studies that highlight the benefits of ethical design on user experience and business success. Can you support me in researching and compiling real-world examples that demonstrate the positive outcomes of prioritizing ethical design principles?

Example Prompt 4:

I'm seeking assistance in gathering case studies that showcase the tangible impact of ethical design choices on user experience and business success. Can you help me identify and analyze examples that illustrate the value of ethical design in creating positive outcomes for both users and companies?

Idea: Accessible Website Design

ChatGPT can provide resources and guidance for creating accessible website designs, ensuring that all users can access and navigate the content.

Example Prompt 1:
Can you provide tips and best practices for creating accessible website designs, including considerations for users with visual impairments and motor disabilities?

Example Prompt 2:
How can I ensure that my website is fully accessible to users with different abilities, and what tools or resources can I use to test for accessibility?

Example Prompt 3:
I'm looking to make my website more inclusive and accessible to all users. Can you help me understand the principles of accessible design and how to implement them effectively?

Example Prompt 4:
I want to create a website that is easy to navigate and use for everyone, regardless of their abilities. Can you provide guidance on designing for accessibility and ensuring a positive user experience for all?

Idea: Ethical Design Certification

ChatGPT can assist in developing a certification program for ethical design, recognizing and promoting ethical design practices within the industry.

Example Prompt 1:
Prompt: "Create a visual identity for our Ethical Design Certification program, incorporating elements that represent integrity, transparency, and responsibility in design practices."

Example Prompt 2:

Prompt: "Design a series of promotional materials for our Ethical Design Certification program, including social media graphics, website banners, and printed materials to raise awareness and encourage participation."

Example Prompt 3:

Prompt: "Develop a set of guidelines and standards for ethical design, with visual examples and case studies that illustrate best practices in user-centered, inclusive, and sustainable design."

Example Prompt 4:

Prompt: "Produce a comprehensive online course on ethical design principles, utilizing engaging visuals and interactive elements to educate and empower designers to integrate ethical considerations into their work."

HOW YOU CAN AUTOMATE PARTS OF YOUR GRAPHIC DESIGNERS JOB

INTRODUCTION

The Significance of Automation
Envision stepping into a workspace of the future—your future —where you're not weighed down by tedious tasks. Where you're liberated to excel at what you do best. Welcome to the future for Graphic Designers, a realm where technology is not just a convenience but a potent force for change. Specifically, we're talking about automation and AI, game-changers that are transforming industries. If you're a Graphic Designer, it's crucial to take notice.

The Goals of this Chapter
The main takeaway? We're not just scratching the surface here. We'll dive deep into the fundamentals of AI and automation, tailored specifically for Graphic Designers. By the end of this chapter, you'll see the horizon of opportunities that can make you more productive, and more importantly, more secure in your job.

How Automation Benefits Graphic Designers
Imagine it: fewer hours spent on manual data entry and more hours for strategic thinking. Sound too good to be true? It's not. Automation is not just a fancy word for tech enthusiasts; it's a tool, available right now, to enhance your work life, make you more efficient, and secure your job.

THE DIFFERENCES BETWEEN AI AND AUTOMATION

Understanding the distinction between automation and AI is crucial for Graphic Designers. Automation tackles the mundane, freeing you up to focus on more creative pursuits. Meanwhile, AI goes a step further by providing intelligent suggestions and even predicting future trends. As a Graphic Designer, mastering the interplay between these two technologies is essential for becoming a champion of automation in your organization.

IMPLEMENTING AI AUTOMATIONS

Now that you have a solid understanding of the background of AI Automation, it's time to roll up your sleeves and get practical. This chapter offers a range of pathways to apply what you've learned, catering to your comfort level, time availability, and resource allocation.

If you're someone who enjoys taking matters into your own hands, you're in for a treat. Meet Zapier and Make.com, two game-changing platforms that act as your own digital task forces, available 24/7 to streamline repetitive tasks and develop custom workflows. Zapier excels at connecting multiple apps you already use, while Make.com offers the flexibility to create more complex processes. The best part? Both platforms are designed for those without a coding background and offer a range of tutorials to help you get started.

If DIY isn't your style or you're short on time, don't worry. There are other excellent options available. Visit my website, jeroenerne.com/aiautomation, for a one-stop hub to outsource your automation needs to specialized companies. These experts can tailor solutions to perfectly align with your business requirements. And if you're eager to advance your automation skill set, the site also offers personal training options to help you elevate your game.

FUTURE-PROOFING YOUR GRAPHIC DESIGNERS ROLE

As a graphic designer, it's natural to wonder if advancing technology will make your skills obsolete. But fear not, this is not a threat to your career, it's an opportunity. By staying ahead of the curve and continuously learning and adapting, you can secure your place in the industry.

Embracing automation and AI doesn't mean your role is in jeopardy; it means it's evolving. In the upcoming chapters, we'll explore a wealth of automation ideas that can propel your company's growth. It's up to you to take the lead. When other companies in your field catch up (and they will), your foresight and action will make you indispensable. So, keep learning, keep adapting, and keep leading the way.

AUTOMATION IDEAS AND CASE STUDIES

With a solid understanding of the basics and a proactive approach, you are ready to embark on the truly game-changing phase of this adventure. This chapter presents you with actionable automation strategies specifically designed for professionals in the field of Graphic Design. These strategies are not just about simplifying your workload; they are about enhancing your company's competitiveness and stability.

SOCIAL MEDIA POST GENERATION

Social media post generation using AI involves the automatic creation of posts with relevant graphics and text based on specific parameters. This technology can help businesses save time and resources while ensuring a consistent and engaging social media presence.

Example:
ABC Company, a leading fashion brand, uses AI-powered social media post generation to create visually stunning posts with compelling captions tailored to their target audience. This automation allows them to maintain a strong online presence and drive customer engagement without the need for manual content creation.

IMAGE EDITING

Image editing | AI can automate tasks such as background removal, color correction, and image resizing, saving time for graphic designers. This technology allows for faster turnaround times and more efficient workflows in the design process.

Fictive example:
XYZ Corp, a leading e-commerce company, implemented AI-powered image editing to streamline their product photography process. By automating tasks such as background removal and color correction, they were able to significantly reduce the time it takes to prepare product images for their website, resulting in faster updates and improved visual consistency across their online store.

TEMPLATE CREATION

Template creation allows graphic designers to use AI to quickly and efficiently create templates for various design projects, such as brochures, flyers, and social media graphics. This automation streamlines the design process and ensures consistency across different marketing materials.

Fictive example:
A marketing agency, XYZ Marketing, has implemented AI-powered template creation to streamline their design process. By using AI, they are able to quickly generate customized templates for their clients' marketing materials, saving time and ensuring a consistent brand image across all platforms. This automation has allowed them to take on more clients and deliver high-quality designs in a shorter amount of time.

DATA VISUALIZATION

Data visualization | AI can be used to automatically generate infographics and data visualizations based on input data, saving time for graphic designers. This technology allows for quick and efficient creation of visually appealing and informative graphics, freeing up designers to focus on more complex and creative tasks.

Fictive example:
XYZ Corp, a leading marketing firm, implemented AI-powered data visualization automation to streamline their reporting process. By inputting client data into the system, the AI generates professional and customized infographics, allowing the design team to spend more time on strategic planning and creative campaigns. This has resulted in faster turnaround times and increased client satisfaction.

FONT PAIRING SUGGESTIONS

Font pairing suggestions | AI can analyze and suggest font pairings based on the design requirements, saving time for graphic designers in the decision-making process. This automation tool can help create cohesive and visually appealing designs by recommending complementary fonts for headings, body text, and other design elements.

Example:
ABC Corp, a leading marketing agency, implemented AI-powered font pairing suggestions to streamline their design process. By using this automation, their graphic designers were able to quickly find the perfect font combinations for their client's branding materials, saving time and ensuring a consistent and professional look across all designs.

AUTOMATED LAYOUT DESIGN

Automated layout design utilizes AI to assist in creating layout designs for various graphic design projects, including print materials and websites. This technology streamlines the design process, saving time and resources while ensuring high-quality results.

Fictive example:
ABC Marketing, a leading digital marketing agency, has implemented automated layout design to streamline their graphic design process. By utilizing AI technology, they are able to create customized and professional layout designs for their clients in a fraction of the time, allowing them to take on more projects and deliver exceptional results.

COLOR PALETTE GENERATION

Color palette generation is a process where AI analyzes images and suggests color palettes based on the content, saving time for graphic designers in the color selection process. This automation tool can quickly generate color schemes that match the theme or mood of an image, making it easier for designers to create visually appealing graphics.

Example:
ABC Design Co. has implemented color palette generation AI to streamline their design process. By using this automation, their designers can quickly generate color schemes for their clients' branding materials, saving time and ensuring that the colors align with the brand's identity. This has allowed the company to increase their productivity and deliver high-quality designs to their clients more efficiently.

AUTOMATED LOGO DESIGN

Automated logo design uses AI to generate logo concepts based on input criteria, giving graphic designers a starting point for their designs. This streamlines the design process and allows for more creativity and efficiency in logo creation.

Fictive example:
A tech startup, XYZ Solutions, implements automated logo design to create a modern and sleek logo for their new software product. They input their brand colors, industry keywords, and desired style, and the AI generates several logo concepts for their designers to work with. This saves time and resources, allowing the team to focus on refining the logo to perfectly represent their brand.

BATCH PROCESSING

Batch processing refers to the automated processing of a large volume of tasks in one go. With the help of AI, batch processing tasks such as resizing, renaming, and organizing large numbers of images can be automated, saving time for graphic designers and streamlining their workflow.

For example, a fictional company called "Creative Solutions" implemented AI-powered batch processing to automate the resizing and renaming of thousands of product images for their e-commerce website. This allowed their graphic designers to focus on more creative tasks, while the AI system efficiently handled the repetitive and time-consuming image processing tasks.

CONTENT GENERATION

Content generation | AI can assist in generating written content for graphic design projects, such as ad copy or social media captions, based on input criteria. This can save time and effort for designers and marketers, while ensuring that the content is tailored to the specific needs of the project.

Fictive example:
A digital marketing agency, XYZ Marketing, implements AI-powered content generation to streamline their graphic design projects. By inputting key details about the target audience and campaign goals, the AI generates ad copy and social media captions that are optimized for engagement and conversion. This allows the agency to focus on the visual aspects of their designs, while the AI handles the written content.

EPILOGUE

As I conclude this handbook on artificial intelligence for graphic designers, I want to express my gratitude to all the readers who have embarked on this journey with me. The world of graphic design is constantly evolving, and the integration of AI technology is revolutionizing the way we approach our work.

In this book, we have explored the capabilities of ChatGPT and how it can be utilized to automate various aspects of the graphic design process. From brainstorming design concepts to organizing digital assets and creating optimized graphics for social media, ChatGPT offers a wealth of possibilities for enhancing our creative output.

I hope that the insights and strategies shared in this book have inspired you to embrace AI as a valuable tool in your design practice. By leveraging the power of ChatGPT, we can streamline our workflows, gain new perspectives, and elevate the quality of our designs.

As we move forward, I encourage you to stay informed about the latest developments in AI for graphic design. You can sign up for my newsletter to receive regular updates and insights on this topic. Additionally, feel free to reach out to me with any questions or feedback through my website.

Thank you once again for joining me on this exploration of AI in graphic design. I wish you all the best in your creative endeavors, and I look forward to continuing this conversation in the future.

Warm regards,
Jeroen Erné

ABOUT THE AUTHOR & COMPLETE AI TRAINING

Jeroen's journey in the field of technology and digital innovation is a profound testament to what passion, dedication, and a forward-thinking mindset can achieve. Not just an individual working in the AI sector, Jeroen stands out as a pioneer, whose initiatives have significantly impacted thousands of individuals across a multitude of professions. At the helm of Nexibeo AI and Complete AI Training, he has been instrumental in demonstrating the transformative potential of integrating AI into our daily workflows, proving that it is not merely a futuristic concept but a tangible, game-changing reality.

Jeroen's commitment to digital innovation has catalyzed the ascent of over a thousand companies to unprecedented levels of success through his leadership at his agencies: JoyGroup Web Design, Nova Interactive, and Nexibeo Development. His ventures as (Co-)Founder of startups like SimplySocial, MobileRevolution, and Coincheckup.com further illustrate his keen insight into the tech landscape and his ability to innovate and drive positive change within it.

Central to Jeroen founded CompleteAiTraining.com in 2023, where his ambition extends beyond mere instruction to the empowerment of professionals. Here, he equips thousands with the knowledge and tools necessary for weaving AI into their daily activities. The platform provides an exhaustive suite of resources tailored to various professions, including custom ChatGPTs, thousands of specific prompts, in-depth courses, video tutorials, audiobooks, eBooks, reference guides, and unlimited inquiries to an AI strategy GPT. These resources are made available through the purchase of his book on platforms like Amazon, which also offers a month of complimentary access to Complete AI Training for further exploration at https://completeaitraining.com/free-resources-amazon.

Jeroen's influence extends well beyond his training platform. Having authored 240 AI-focused books for a broad spectrum of professions, he has armed a myriad of individuals with the capabilities to seamlessly integrate AI into their work environments. These publications are accessible on Amazon (https://www.amazon.com/stores/author/B0CKRXVNB2) and via subscriptions on CompleteAITraining.com.

With Jeroen guiding Nexibeo AI, the company plays a crucial role in helping businesses incorporate AI into their daily operations effectively, ensuring they remain leaders in innovation.

Jeroen is more than an author or an entrepreneur; he is a visionary who is pushing the boundaries in the technology, AI, and innovation sectors. His journey and insights can be followed on LinkedIn at https://www.linkedin.com/in/jeroenerne/.

His narrative is not just about the accomplishments of an individual but highlights the capacity of AI to revolutionize our world—making it more intelligent, efficient, and interconnected. Jeroen's work is about simplifying complexity, making innovation practical, and bringing the future within our reach, one step at a time.

Could you help me grow

with a Review?

Hello, amazing reader, may I ask you for a favor? I hope you've found valuable insights and enjoyed your journey through the pages of this AI handbook, dedicated to you. If you feel inspired, I'd be truly thrilled if you could spare a moment to share your experience on Amazon or wherever you purchased your copy. Your feedback not only brightens our day—it also helps others discover the book's value. So, could you kindly light up the stars with your review? Thank you for being so awesome and for all your support!